PRESENTING
Sue Ellen Bridgers

TUSAS 563

Twayne's United States Authors Series
Young Adult Authors

Patricia J. Campbell, General Editor

The Young Adult Authors books seek to meet the
need for critical studies of fiction for young adults.
Each volume examines the life and work of one
author, helping both teachers and readers of young
adult literature to understand better the writers they
have read with such pleasure and fascination.

PRESENTING

Sue Ellen Bridgers

Ted Hipple

Twayne Publishers • Boston
A Division of G. K. Hall & Co.

Presenting Sue Ellen Bridgers
Ted Hipple

Copyright 1990 by G. K. Hall & Co.
All rights reserved.
Published by Twayne Publishers
A division of G. K. Hall & Co.
70 Lincoln Street
Boston, Massachusetts 02111

Copyediting supervised by Barbara Sutton.
Book production by Janet Z. Reynolds.
Typeset by Crane Typesetting Service, West Barnstable, Massachusetts.

Printed on permanent/durable acid-free paper
and bound in the United States of America.

First published 1990.
10 9 8 7 6 5 4 3 2 1

Library of Congress Cataloging-in-Publication Data

Hipple, Ted.
    Presenting Sue Ellen Bridgers / Ted Hipple.
        p.   cm. — (Twayne's United States authors series ; TUSAS
563. Young adult authors)
    Includes bibliographical references.
    ISBN 0-8057-8213-3 (alk. paper)
    1. Bridgers, Sue Ellen—Criticism and interpretation. 2. Young
adult fiction, American—History and criticism. I. Title.
II. Series: Twayne's United States authors series ; TUSAS 563.
III. Series: Twayne's United States authors series. Young adult
authors.
PS3552.R4543Z69 1990
813'.54—dc20   89-77329
                                                          CIP

Contents

Preface

Sue Ellen Bridgers is an outstanding writer. Like many of her contemporaries in the field of young adult literature today, she writes realistic novels in which adolescent characters are confronted with lifelike and significant problems. What sets her apart from other authors and makes her worth reading and study are the excellence of her writing and the wisdom and vision she brings to bear on that writing. Readers who like Bridgers's novels sense their integrity, their commitment, their intelligence. They also value her choice to explore the lives of ordinary people—people, after all, not unlike the readers of her books. Whether we believe, with Thoreau, that most of us live lives of quiet desperation, the fact remains that few of us become international spies or Hollywood stars or even win the crucial game with a spectacular touchdown. Most of us are, as it happens, ordinary.

These are the folk whose stories Bridgers tells. The characters she creates are rural, far away from the big cities where exciting things often seem to happen. But she is able to demonstrate that exciting things can also happen in small-town North Carolina. She places her adolescent characters in contexts that extend well beyond their peer groups, beyond even the lives of their parents and teachers, to include much older people, particularly grandparents. And she does it all with extraordinary skill, an ability that goes from choosing the right word or phrase to developing an entire plot line that keeps readers turning pages.

In her novel *Permanent Connections* Bridgers describes Ginny Collier, a marvelously drawn and complex woman who soothes some of her troubled emotions by weaving at a large loom in her mountain cabin. Though very different from Ginny, Bridgers is herself a weaver—of stories, characters, themes, and settings— and these divisions seemed to develop naturally in my thinking about the organization of this book. Rather than take her novels serially and treat each one as a separate entity, I sought and found common threads and have been able to weave these together in chapters devoted to story, character, theme, and setting. Framing these chapters are a beginning biographical chapter on the writer herself and an ending one that explores her writing somewhat more technically. In this final chapter, too, is an attempt to place Bridgers's work in the context of both other novelists for young adults and other Southern authors.

Many people deserve acknowledgment for their signal contributions to whatever merit this volume has, most of all Sue Ellen Bridgers herself. A gracious hostess at her rural North Carolina home while we talked—my tape recorder going, my note-taking pen busy—she has since that time been willing to respond to letters and to telephone requests for even more information. I am indebted to Patricia J. Campbell, the general editor of Twayne's United States Authors Series: Young Adult Authors, and to Liz T. Fowler, the in-house editor in Boston, who both helped me immeasurably. I wrote this book with a word processor, thanks to two persons with whom I work daily who convinced me that there is life beyond the fountain pen. Debbie Bain is a senior secretary in the Department of Curriculum and Instruction at the University of Tennessee and Claudia Ferguson is that department's head secretary and administrative services assistant. To them I owe much. I want also to thank my wife, Marjorie, for her rigorous editorial help and for her encouragement and generosity of spirit about the whole project.

Additionally I must mention the nameless thousands, some of whom I have seen, most of whom I'll never know, who are the young people and adults who read Sue Ellen Bridgers's novels. They are assigned them in English classes, check them out of school and public libraries, buy them at bookstores. It is their continuing and growing interest in what she has achieved that makes books like this one appropriate.

Ted Hipple

University of Tennessee

Chronology

1942 Sue Ellen Hunsucker born 20 September in Winterville, North Carolina.

1960 Enters East Carolina State College.

1963 Marries Ben Bridgers; moves to Mississippi; daughter Elizabeth Abbott born.

1966 Moves to South Dakota; daughter Jane Bennett born.

1968 Moves to Chapel Hill, North Carolina; son Sean MacKenzie born.

1971 Moves to Sylva, North Carolina; publishes short stories in little magazines.

1975 Enrolls in Western Carolina University.

1976 *Home Before Dark*; graduates with highest honors from Western Carolina University.

1979 *All Together Now.*

1981 *Notes for Another Life.*

1985 Receives ALAN Award for "Distinguished Contributions to Young Adult Literature"; *Sara Will.*

1987 *Permanent Connections.*

1989 Papers placed in special archives in Hunter Library at Western Carolina University.

1. A Writer's Life

She was about twelve years of age. Sue Ellen Hunsucker and her mother were driving and had stopped for a traffic light. The youngster mused on her future, speculating about whether she would be a teacher or an engineer or perhaps a nurse. "Oh, Sue Ellen," her mother said, with just enough impatience in her voice to suggest that this matter had long been settled, "you are going to be a writer." Bridgers ends this report of her mother's gentle insistence with the simple sentence: "And so I am."[1]

And so she is a writer—of short stories (some earlier in her career, a few recently), of articles and speeches (about her writing), and of novels (five at present). It is the novels that have earned her both considerable critical acclaim and continuing appreciation from readers of many ages and intellects, a sizable number of them adolescents. By her lights she writes for all readers, for whoever comes along, and there have been many of these people; her books have sold well. Yet the considerable critical attention she has been given suggests that her most faithful audience is composed of young adults and their teachers and librarians. In schools her books have been purchased in classroom sets for readings in common and are often used by students for their book reports. In organizations like ALAN (the Assembly on Literature for Adolescents of the National Council of Teachers of English) that are devoted to the study of young adult literature she is a well-known author, the subject of serious articles and convention presentations. In book sections of newspapers and journals under headings like "new books for older children" her novels are regularly reviewed, usually favorably.

Unlike many of her author colleagues in this field of adolescent literature, however, Bridgers does not limit her young adult novels principally to teenagers and their concerns, with adults consigned to shadowy background roles. Joseph Milner points out that she seems out of step with her fellow writers in that she presents her teenagers and their families "both vertically and horizontally,"[2] giving them brothers and sisters and age-mate friends but, at the same time, aunts and uncles and, particularly, grandparents. Though her novels feature adolescents in central roles, they are written from an omniscient third-person point of reference that facilitates her exploration of the actions and thoughts of all her characters, including the older ones. These shifts in voice seem self-indulgent to some critics, yet they widen the scope of her novels to include many figures beyond the teenagers. And they reflect the importance in her own life of what Milner calls a "vertical" family.

For Bridgers's roots go deep. And she has elected to use her background in her writing, not autobiographically but as a source, as a point of departure. The kind of small town she was reared in and still lives in provides the setting for her novels, which portray older women in important roles and explore relationships among the characters in vertical families. The grandmothers in such novels as *All Together Now* and *Notes for Another Life* share the wisdom, the decency, the commitment to home and hearth, the love for their grandchildren that the young Sue Ellen experienced with her own grandmothers in rural North Carolina. Her characters are rural people; it is her mission to illuminate and, when possible, praise their lives. Her themes are equally rural in nature. Somewhat fixed, then, in space, in characterizations, in philosophy, she nonetheless manages to write compellingly interesting books that are masterly exemplars of the author's craft.

Bridgers's Early Life

One can begin with Bridgers's life almost before its beginning, with her great-grandmother, whose involvement with Sue Ellen borders on the supernatural. Let Bridgers tell the story:

> My earliest memory is of my great-grandmother McGlohan. For most of my life I believed I had dreamed of being with her, of seeing her at a distance and then closer and closer until I was looking up at her. This face looking down into mine is crystal clear to me, as if it is a photographic image locked in my brain. Only recently did I discover that this vision of her was not a dream at all but a recurrent happening. Almost every day when I was a baby, my mother carried me down the hall to the room where my great-grandmother was bedridden. I would lie on the bed next to her and she would talk and play with me. I was only eighteen months old when she died.[3]

Other powerful memories of her young life inform what she is, what she does, and what she writes: the tobacco farms of eastern North Carolina, her father's frequent incapacitating bouts with mental illness, the love and support of her mother, the stories she overheard her grandmothers share, the civility that seems still to be more pervasive in the little towns Bridgers grew up in than in the nation's urban centers. Arguably, all authors are products of their past; no possible dissent exists in Bridgers's case.

That past began in Winterville, North Carolina, on 20 September 1942, when the third child of Bett Abbott and Wayland Hunsucker was born and named Sue Ellen, in honor of her Aunt Sue, whose birthday she shares. Older sister Sandra Elizabeth, today a North Carolina teacher of English, was two years of age at Sue Ellen's birth. Before their births another sister had died in early infancy. Because Winterville was a small town, because both her grandmothers were still active, vital women who lived nearby, because her father and mother had numerous siblings who themselves had children, the vertical and horizontal families extended far. Aunts, uncles, cousins were everywhere.[4]

But it was grandmothers who made the lasting impression. They told her stories. (Today she says that her maternal grandmother Abbott was the real storyteller in the Abbott-Hunsucker-Bridgers lineage.) Often their stories centered on their own mothers, including Sue Ellen's great-grandmother. They told of how these women and their siblings would gather on their porches of a night, quilting pieces in their hands, to sew and talk. Bridgers would like to have been there, not as fellow conversationalist, but as listener: "Oh, to have been privy to those words spoken in the quiet of early evening, to have hung on the silences that hovered between them like smoke."[5]

And so young Sue Ellen grew up among storytellers—her grandmothers, but also her books. She became ill at age three with what at that time was believed to be rheumatic fever and for the next two years led a somewhat sheltered existence, one in which she listened intently to the stories told by her mother and her grandmothers and to the books they read to her. Then came first grade, where she learned to read. She became an active participant in the wonderful world of books, a world she has never left and of which she feels proud yet humble to be part. Favorites included Winnie the Pooh and his friends and *The Little Engine That Could*. She even recalls two stories she did not like and still does not like: *The Three Little Pigs* and *The Little Rabbit Who Wanted Red Wings*. These are, she says, "separation stories" that lack a divine hand to rescue the characters. She would listen breathlessly to the little rabbit story, to "the horrible circumstances that surrounded not being recognized by one's own mother."[6] Curiously, her writing today frequently features adolescents separated from their mothers. The difference may be the hand hovering protectively over them—Bridgers's own hand.

School also introduced her to writing. Even in first grade she wrote poems and stories and continued throughout her schooling the practice of writing whenever she could, not simply assignments for classes but also pieces for her own pleasure. Winterville's nearest large city is Raleigh and when Bridgers was in high school one of its newspapers published a daily poem. Many of them were hers, providing, if not money, at least the heady stimulation that comes from seeing one's name in print and knowing that one's writings may be read by unknown others. Her first earnings as a teenager went toward a typewriter and, when she was pecking away, her mother would tell her friends that Sue Ellen was busy and would see them later. Writing thus had a legitimacy, an importance. It was worth doing.

Yet not all was sweetness and light, kindly grandmothers, good grades, cheerleading, and band trips when Bridgers was a child. Her father, earlier a central Winterville political figure, its mayor for a few years, and a moderately successful tobacco farmer, became mentally unstable. Her discussions of that time recall not only her naturally mixed emotions as a teenager with an incapacitated father but also her mother's extraordinary strength. It was her mother who held the family together during that time of crisis. Sue Ellen, her older sister, and brother Abbott, six years her junior, had the legitimate and time-consuming needs of growing children, and their mother met these needs. For fifteen years her father was in and out of mental institutions, undergoing shock treatments, coming home for brief periods when all were optimistic about his chances for recovery, succeeding for short periods as a tobacco farmer, then slipping into a new bout of depression and being returned to the hospital to begin the cycle again. Though living under tremendous stress herself, Bridgers's mother maintained her own balance and her commitment that her children should lead lives as nearly normal as possible. Sue Ellen did. She got the expected good grades in school, led cheers at athletic events, sang in the church choir, had many good friends, and, through it all, continued with the writing that was becoming increasingly important to her.

Given these emotionally wrenching childhood and teenage experiences, it is little wonder that among her most powerful portrayals are the mental illness of Tom in *Notes for Another Life* and the reactions to that illness of Tom's mother Bliss, his wife Karen, and, most of all, his children Kevin and Wren. Bridgers even assigns to Kevin fears that she had when she was his age, and still has today, that the mental illness of the father will appear in the child.

When her father was home and if not well, at least better, he worked long and hard hours in the tobacco fields and barns. It was her homemaker mother who provided Sue Ellen with the consistent emotional support and love that shaped her upbringing. That support and love still exist; Bridgers and her mother are close and see each other often. Her father died in 1985.

College, Marriage, Family

A good student in high school, a fine writer even then, one for whom English teachers provided special assignments and attention, Bridgers was graduated in 1960 and that fall went to nearby East Carolina State College (now East Carolina University), twenty miles from Winterville, the school her mother had attended years earlier. There both her writing and her life blossomed. This literary and personal expansion began in her first week of college, when she, a small-town girl still, had the temerity to apply to be on the staff of the college literary magazine, which, she says, has no peer "for snobbery, pomposity, ego-tripping, and scorched coffee."[7] She volunteered to be a typist. Yet it was not long before she realized that she could write poems and stories as good as those she was typing. She sent in one of her own. It was accepted. Sue Ellen Bridgers had hit the big time.

In her junior year of college Mac Hyman, the novelist who had written the best-selling *No Time for Sergeants*, came to ECSC as writer-in-residence and shared an office with Ben Bridgers, an English instructor from the Southwest who was then twenty-three. Sue Ellen met Hyman and, through him, Ben. Their shared interests in literature and the academic life led to shared interests in everything and, in the spring of the next year, 1963, Sue Ellen and Ben were married during the break between quarters. That next quarter was Ben's last as a college instructor, however. Burned out by academic life, he decided, with Sue Ellen's complete support, to follow Hyman's advice and join the Air Force. Sue Ellen left college without completing her degree. The next year

A portrait of the Bridgers in their family room (*left to right*): Sue Ellen, daughter Elizabeth, daughter Bennett, husband Ben, son Sean.

Bett Abbot Hunsucker, Sue Ellen's mother, with her daughters Sandra, four, and Sue Ellen, two.

Sue Ellen at four.

Sue Ellen as a high school
senior.

The Bridgers family (*left to right*): daughter Elizabeth, Sue Ellen, husband Ben, son Sean, daughter Bennett.

they were living in Mississippi. Daughter Elizabeth Abbott was born there.

The following year came a move to Rapid City, South Dakota, and Ben's service duty on a Strategic Air Command base. And another child came, too, Jane Bennett. By then Ben had decided to enroll in law school at the University of North Carolina at Chapel Hill. There he worked two jobs, while Sue Ellen tended two baby girls. A third child, Sean MacKenzie, was born in 1968. With a husband in law school, three children under five, and an apartment to keep in the domestic tradition in which she had been reared, Sue Ellen found that time for writing simply did not exist.

After Ben graduated, the family's search for a place to settle ended in their discovery of Sylva, a small town in the far western tip of North Carolina, close to Smoky Mountain National Park. It met their "basic requirements": a job for Ben, a college for Sue Ellen, and an Episcopal Church for all of them.[8]

Bridgers's Short Stories

Son Sean joined his two older sisters in school shortly after the move to Sylva and Bridgers found that she could return to college on a part-time basis and to writing. She published short stories in small literary magazines that gave authors complimentary copies as payment. The work on these stories provided a kind of training ground for her as a writer, an opportunity to learn that, for her, character development is the essential element in fiction, the one to which all other aspects of storytelling must be subordinated. In these stories she sharpened her skills as a painter of verbal portraits, skills that are evident in all of her novels. Yet there are other similarities between these early stories and the later novels. The stories were placed in small-town North Carolina. The themes that would later inform her longer works took root in these stories. Love and the importance of families, particularly vertical families, were common thematic explorations.

A brief description of three of the stories will illustrate what Bridgers was feeling and thinking at that time and how closely the stories she wrote then parallel the novels she writes today. "The World that Winter"[9] appeared in 1971 in *Crucible* magazine. In that story teenaged Margaret befriends aged "Aunt" Lucy, really no relation to her but a good friend of Margaret's recently deceased grandmother. A widow, with a son in faraway Seattle, set in her ways, living out life on its own terms, Lucy reappears years later as Sara Will in the novel of that name. The connection between a teenager and an older woman who provides matter-of-fact wisdom and love, here the central theme of a three-page story, was to become one of the dominant elements in every one of Bridgers's novels.

Another story came out three years later in that same small literary magazine and, again, Sue Ellen Bridgers explored the life of an older woman. Even then she was moving toward the goal that continues to influence much of her thinking—the study of women, often older women, in their connections to the ones they love. "I Call This Place Mine"[10] opens with Rosalie, fifty-one and widowed, awaiting the return home of her only child, Danny, who had earlier called to say he had married someone the previous day, someone Rosalie did not know, did not even know about. The shock almost wrecks her ordered life—she even forgets to call and get a substitute for the bridge game she will miss—and the meeting with Danny and his bride Patty does not go smoothly. A woman who has submerged so much of her life, first for her husband, later for her son, Rosalie nonetheless has a child so thoughtless that he cannot even tell her before the fact that he is getting married. Patty at least has the grace to say that, if she were in Rosalie's shoes, she would be hurt and angry. Ever the supportive mother, Rosalie tries to protect Danny, yet the future of this threesome seems highly problematic.

In this same story Bridgers provided an early demonstration of her considerable power with language and her deft use of descriptions, particularly of women's homes. Rosalie's living room could later have been Maggie's in *Home before Dark* or Jane's in *All Together Now* or Sara Will's:

The room looked perfect. It was filled with comfortable, used things, but wasn't in the least shabby. She stood for a moment looking at it—the Lawson sofa, the over-stuffed chairs covered in striped velvet, the piano with sheet music in careful disarray, the book cases full of old volumes but sprinkled with a few new ones she'd bought to bring out the color, the tables gleaming with lemon oil, the oriental rugs. Between the book cases was a large window reaching the ceiling, shimmering with translucent curtains. Beneath the window was a seat cushioned with worn, supple leather.[11]

Between the publication of these stories was the 1972 printing of "All Summer Dying" in the *Carolina Quarterly*.[12] Perhaps the most obviously autobiographical piece Bridgers has written, it details the events leading up to the death of a teenage girl's grandfather: his severe stroke, his forgetting the names of his many grandchildren, his frequent wandering away from the safety of his home. Margaret and her mother find him in their small Carolina town and return him to his wife, Margaret's patient if stubborn grandmother. All the women understand that the patterns will probably be repeated until the old man's death.

Though it means leaping ahead chronologically, a brief examination of two recently published stories can complete this discussion of Bridgers as a writer of short stories. Donald Gallo has assembled three volumes of original short stories by noted authors of young adult fiction; Bridgers's work has appeared in two of them. In *Visions* her story is "The Beginning of Something."[13] The setting is typical Bridgers—rural North Carolina. Again, she mixes adolescents with their horizontal and vertical families. Teenager Roseanne is traveling across the state to the funeral of Cousin Jessie, her mother's relative and best friend, just as Roseanne and Jessie's daughter Melissa are good friends. The funeral is described, with a number of adult reactions portrayed. But what really happens that weekend is that Roseanne gets her first kiss from a friend of Melissa's boyfriend. After the funeral Roseanne thinks, "I'm going to tell Melissa how sorry I am. I'm going to tell Cousin Roy [Melissa's father], too, because I haven't told him yet. But I'm not going to tell anybody about

Travis Cuthbert kissing me. It's as private as grief but it doesn't need sharing."[14]

Gallo's next collection, *Connections*, features another Bridgers story, this one a continuation of the previous one. In "Life's a Beach"[15] Cousin Roy has remarried, only six months after Jessie's death, to the tearful chagrin of Roseanne's mother. Still, they must accept the generous offer of Roy's new bride that Roseanne come to spend the summer at the beach house with Melissa. There she and Melissa go after the same boy, Scott, Roseanne feeling sure that she will lose; after all, Melissa is prettier, quicker witted, more experienced. Yet it is she—Roseanne—whom Scott likes.

But Bridgers as a writer of short stories, then and now, is no match for Bridgers as a writer of novels, in her own estimation or that of her many readers. And, in 1976, Bridgers became a novelist. That year was for her one of those banner years when things happen in such a way that life can never again be the same. In that one twelve-month period Bridgers realized two major goals: she published a novel and she graduated from college. The college work was completed at Western Carolina University in Cullowhee, about five miles from Sylva, an easy commute for the writer with a family at home. WCU sits rather majestically atop a tall hill, though its recent growth has caused it to spread to the adjacent flatlands, and it gave Bridgers an education she is pleased with. She majored in English, graduated with honors, and made friendships with faculty and staff that exist yet today.

Home before Dark was also published that year. A condensed version of it first appeared in *Redbook*, where Bridgers had earlier published short stories. Ann Smith, *Redbook*'s fiction editor, suggested to Bridgers that she send the work to Pat Ross, fiction editor at Knopf. It was Ross who made the classification that changed Bridgers's life and her novels: she selected *Home before Dark* for the Knopf Young Adult Division, a move that surprised the author but one she refers to today as a "great career move." (Her next two novels, *All Together Now* and *Notes for Another Life*, also went to Ross at Knopf, but then Ross left and Bridgers acquired a New York City agent, Elaine Markson, with whom she still works.)

The publication of *Home before Dark* was truly an exciting time for all of the Bridgers family. Sue Ellen's husband and children knew for certain then that she was a serious writer, one to be reckoned with. Ben, himself a person of letters, perhaps most shared Sue Ellen's joy, but the children, too, were aware that their mother had made a quantum leap from the short stories she had produced before. She took on, for a while, the family status of semi-celebrity.

One additional outcome made the publication of *Home before Dark* special. The Bridgers were able to use the money Sue Ellen earned from the book for a family trip to England. It was, Bridgers thinks, a great way to spend the royalties, as it provided a kind of tangible experience, a memorable one, for the entire family. (Subsequent royalties have gone for more mundane things —college tuition, house repairs.)

Bridgers Today

In more ways than not the Sue Ellen Bridgers who published *Home before Dark* in 1976 resembles the Sue Ellen Bridgers of today, four novels later. She still lives in Sylva, where Ben's law practice has flourished concurrently with her literary career. They still live in a many-roomed, rambling house made private by a large, tree-filled lot. The largest room, a converted two-car garage, is an ideal family room—big, with overstuffed chairs and couches to seat ten or more, two huge picture windows looking out on the always-colorful Carolina countryside, a corner stereo, a hidden and, one suspects, infrequently used television set, and everywhere books, rather too neatly alphabetized. "It's Ben's doing," Bridgers says. And then the visitor notices on one wall, in a break in the bookshelves, a large portrait that seems disquietingly familiar. A second glance tells why. It is a picture of that very room, with five inhabitants, the Bridgers family, all adults, looking comfortably relaxed, "at home."

But they are all at home only on occasion now. Daughter Elizabeth graduated from Oglethorpe College and works in Atlanta. Daughter Jane Bennett, called by her middle name, graduated from Hampshire College and is considering graduate school. Sean lives at home, at least for a time, while attending nearby Western Carolina University in Cullowhee, but he spends long days on campus, where he often has lead roles in dramatic productions. All three children majored in English in college, a powerful testimony to the magic of language and literature in their lives and their parents'. Ben has an office about a mile from their house. Two quiet companions roam from kitchen to pantry to family room to bedroom to Bridgers's office down the hall: the Tabby Point cats Sara Will and Swanee Hope. (Yes, those *are* the names of the principal women in her novel *Sara Will*.) During most days the house is Bridgers's alone, in the daylight hours at least, hours she spends in writing—when, that is, she is actually writing.

For novels are a three-year activity for her, not all of which is spent in putting words on paper. The first year is her "thinking time," a year when she gets to know as much about the characters she will write about as she can and when she discovers the beginning and ending she plans for them. She does not write then. Not always does she know the middle of her novels in advance of putting anything into the word processor, but, having gotten inside her characters, she has confidence in them and in herself that the middle part will work out. After a year of thinking comes a year of writing. And then a year of the publishing process, including some rather minimal editing; she revises as she goes along and sends her publisher a "fairly clean and final" manuscript.

Bridgers travels frequently, especially during the years when she is not spending two or three hours each morning at the computer. She is often asked to speak to groups like the National Council of Teachers of English, the International Reading Association, or the American Library Association. She is an outstanding platform personality, usually charming her audiences both by what she says and by how she says it. For such occasions she discards the sweat suits she wears at home for a tailored suit, silk blouse, high-heeled shoes. More recently, however, she reports that her out-of-the-house "businesswear" has taken on a more informal aspect, carefully coordinated sweaters and skirts, for example.

In any kind of outfit Bridgers is compellingly attractive, the kind of woman one notices. She looks more athletic than in fact she is, appearing naturally conditioned, fit. Brunette hair frames an even-featured face that breaks easily and often into a winning smile. Her eyes twinkle. But her most commanding aspect is something that is not really physical: one senses almost instantly that Bridgers is smart. She *looks* quick, intelligent.

A few minutes' conversation with Bridgers reinforces this notion. She answers questions thoughtfully, wisely. She talks more often than not in complete sentences, without the interrupting "well's" and "you know's" that plague the speech of many Americans, including writers. One senses that she knows what is going on and how she fits into it, as writer, as woman. She has style, not only on paper but also in person.

There is no brittle sophistication, no pomposity, in Bridgers's makeup. She is down-home, comfortable, relaxed. Her life and her life-style are proof positive that the modern Southern woman is, the stereotypes notwithstanding, neither a flighty ball of fluff held over from Scarlet O'Hara days nor a barefoot hillbilly with a corncob pipe in the corner of her mouth. Instead, Bridgers offers a personal picture of a modern, handsome, peaceful woman who happens to choose to live in the South.

Her reading habits support this view of a modern woman. She regularly reads the *New Yorker* ("and usually more than just the cartoons"), the *New York Times Book Review*, the *Washington Post Weekly*, and the *North Carolina Arts Journal*. A charter subscriber to *Ms.*, she still has every copy of that magazine. Of particular interest to her are its letters columns, as these, she says, provide her with good information about what today's women are thinking and feeling about the issues that confront them. Bridgers has some ambivalence about the term "young adult novel" and does not regularly read the works in that market, though, of course, she keeps up with the acclaimed novelists in the genre: Judy

Blume, S. E. Hinton, Paul Zindel, and, a special favorite, Katherine Paterson. Among novelists who write mainly for adults she is "passionate about" Anne Tyler, with whom she clearly shares a writer's interest in the development of character, and Reynolds Price, with whom she clearly shares a writer's interest in the South.

Neither television nor the movies capture much of Bridgers's attention, though she does confess to a fondness for old movies. Her movie-going tends to increase when she is in her "writing year," as these trips can give her a "quick fix" into someone else's creativity. During this period of intense writing she does not have the time to indulge in a longish novel, but still she needs to see how another imaginative person has put together a scene or populated it with convincing characters. What television she watches similarly reflects her interest in people more than plots. She watches continuing dramas like "L. A. Law" and "thirtysomething," shows that she feels allow her to get inside another writer's depiction of a character. These shows teach her something.

In Sylva Bridgers is well known, but only partly for her novels. "Sure," she says, "when my books come out, people here read them and say something to me about them when I'm in the supermarket. And the local paper comments on my writing." But during the three or four years between novels she will be as frequently approached about her work for the local (and very small) Episcopal Church in Sylva, or for the town's active League of Women Voters chapter, which is attempting to build a fine small-town library. A bit hesitant about the label "feminist," she nonetheless subscribes to the goals of modern women trying to cope with home and job, with future dreams and past obligations. Her circle of close friends includes several women with lives similar to hers— marriages that interrupted college studies, children born almost immediately, husbands' careers that dictated family decisions, delayed personal and professional fulfillment. With several of these women Bridgers formed a consciousness-raising group in the middle seventies. Two of them joined her in returning to college.

To this college, Western Carolina, Bridgers has remained a

faithful and supportive alumna. WCU has returned the friendship and is now readying space for the "Sue Ellen Bridgers papers." It is a fitting tribute to this woman, this neighbor, this author who so honors her region, her education, and her background in all of her novels.

2. The Storyteller

Novelists tell stories. True, they also create settings that we can visualize, fill these with characters that we can like or dislike, and explore themes that we can make our own judgments about, but it often remains their stories that we remember most, that have, if not the most enduring appeal, at least the initial one. "What's it about?" we are asked, and we begin our response with "It's a story. . . ."

Sue Ellen Bridgers tells stories. Though her settings, her characters, her themes also command our attention, we must begin with her stories. It is in them that the settings become actual places, the characters begin breathing, the themes take on larger significances. The five novels that are the focus of this volume, even in the briefest of summaries, reveal that Sue Ellen Bridgers is indeed a storyteller of consummate skill.

Home before Dark

Bridgers's first novel (1976) opens with the Willis family moving from a station wagon to a home of their own. James Earl Willis, his downtrodden and fearful wife Mae, and their children Stella, William, Earl, and baby Lissy, have lived the life of migrant workers, traveling from harvest to harvest, mostly in Florida, living in workers' cottages, sleeping in their battered station wagon between jobs, receiving formal education and medical attention and familial support more when they were convenient than when they were necessary or helpful.

But that life is behind them now, at least temporarily. James Earl has brought his wife and children to his old homestead in rural North Carolina, the family tobacco farm now run by his younger brother, Newton, who became head of the Willis family when James Earl left it for the armed services and, later, life on the road. And on this homestead there is an empty tenant cottage, decrepit, in need of paint and repair, but it will do as a roof for James Earl, a jail for Mae, a palace for fourteen-year-old Stella.

Newton's wife Anne graciously smooths over the awkward beginnings for her newly found inlaws and senses in Stella a young woman of substance and dreams, with a fierce hold on reality and an awareness of her need to fashion her own life. Mae, Anne realizes, feels trapped in this new way of living, worn down by fears of eating with the wrong fork, scared that James Earl may settle in to a tenant farmer's life, missing the migrant rootlessness that permitted her to escape responsibility and commitment.

Soon the two families exist side by side. James Earl and Newton replace their initial hesitancy with genuine brotherly affection born in shared twelve-hour days in the tobacco fields. James Earl realizes that "now I'm home and that counts for something" (21). Stella and new friend Toby paint the shack where they live and, with Anne's help, turn a house into a home. Life seems directed, centered. And yet not for Mae, who replies to Stella's wish to stay with Newton and Anne forever, "There ain't no forever. We keep moving 'cause that's what we can do" (19). But even Mae soon comes to know that "what was a beginning for her child was a final, desperate failure for herself" (20).

During Stella's first date with Toby, she meets slightly older Rodney Biggers, a loner, yet rich and usually in possession of his mother's car. To Toby's jealous but well-founded concern and dismay Stella and Rodney begin to date. Anne becomes the mother Mae never was—advising the young woman on clothes, helping her buy her first bra, keeping a keen eye out for her when she is with Rodney. For Anne, Stella possesses a wildness, a "spirit that Anne had never had and which attracted her. How she admired the way Stella took on life, flipping her head as if beckoning a challenge" (73). Toby recognizes these same qualities in Stella and announces his boyish love for her in a counterproductive way by disparaging Rodney's interest. She continues to see Rodney and to regard Toby as her best friend, but not her boyfriend.

In a freak lightning storm, with all the women working in the tobacco barn, Mae Willis is killed, ending an empty life lived amid sorrows and distress. She had not settled into daily existence on the tobacco farm the way her family had and she had been often too timidly fearful to voice her frequent objections: " 'I despise your goddamned tobacco,' she wanted to say" (88). But she could not.

Though they had loved her as wife and mother, both James Earl and Stella have long suffered her brooding presence and her persistent and almost willful unhappiness. They could never have admitted, even to themselves, that her death provided a kind of release for them, a chance to live fuller lives. Indeed, they wonder if Mae had wanted to die as a final self-abnegating measure to secure their freedom. No longer would Stella and James Earl have to apologize for feeling happy about their new lives. They could forget their guilty twinges about preferring their settled existence in North Carolina to the rootlessness of the migrant life that had complemented Mae's insecurities.

On the night of the funeral Toby sympathetically and lovingly kisses Stella, an act seen by the spying Rodney, who then uses his riches to hire two roughnecks to beat Toby. They overdo it, nearly killing him. Toby's refusal to tell on Rodney, almost as if he believes he had the beating coming, does not fool Stella. She breaks immediately with the crestfallen Rodney, telling him she never wants to see him again despite his repentant protestations that he had only wanted to get Toby to leave Stella alone, not to injure him seriously. But Stella has the final word: "Just get off this porch, Rodney Biggers. . . . You just stay off my property" (136). The "my" speaks volumes about Stella's growth into young adulthood.

Paralleling Stella's own romantic involvements is James Earl's attention to Maggie Grover, the local old-maid owner of the general store and an age-mate of James Earl. It is soon after Mae's funeral, too soon, some in the small town might say, for James Earl to express his interest in courting the eager and sensible Maggie. Their adult companionship leads to a marriage that, to Stella, is wrong, not because of any echo of disrespect for Mae but because it might mean that Stella may have to leave *her* cottage on the Willis homestead and move into town to the Grover house, where James Earl and the other Willis children will live. In town also James Earl will assume a major role in Maggie's business. Even though she is only fifteen years old, Stella flatly refuses to move and, after the wedding, stays on alone at the tenant farm.

A wise Anne and a patient and understanding Maggie finally combine to help Stella change her mind. She realizes that at Maggie's she can have her school friends, including Toby, over for an afternoon of play, an evening of study. And with perceptive maturity and an awareness that she has been selfish she realizes that families must stay together to be truly families. The love she bears for James Earl and now, through him, for Maggie she can best reveal by being near them. She arrives at their place before dark.

Though not always charitable to first-time novelists, critics found in *Home before Dark* a reason to rave. Mary K. Chelton wrote "This is the female coming-of-age story we have waited for and probably the best teen novel I've ever read."[1] Sheila Schwartz, later to become a young adult novelist herself, echoed Chelton: "This is one of the most beautiful adolescent literature books to come my way. I cannot praise too highly its originality, integrity, and power to renew the reader's belief in the goodness of people."[2] Bridgers's fellow North Carolinian Lucy Milner, writing for North Carolina English teachers, called it "well wrought and filled with such hope and humanity that it argues well for classroom use. Students will come away both instructed and delighted."[3] An *English Journal* article labeled the novel a "classic" and ended its tribute with this praise: "Flawlessly written and loaded, like the great Southern novels, with gothic humor and fascinating characters, *Home before Dark* is a likely candidate for the young adult novel teenagers and adults will read for years to come."[4] Clearly the stage was set for a positive critical reception for Bridgers's next novel.

All Together Now

Published in 1979, *All Together Now* provides parallel stories of four relationships. Casey's grandparents Jane and Ben are happily married, and have been for years. Her uncle Taylor's roving and restless period may soon come to an end if his girlfriend Gwen has her way. Pansy and Hazard, the best friends of Casey's grandparents, have loved each other for twenty-five years, but had not married until the summer described in the novel. And the strangest relationship of all is that between Casey, a twelve-year-old girl, and Dwayne, a retarded adult of thirty-three who thinks Casey is a boy. These interwoven stories come together during Casey's summer stay with her grandparents in rural North Carolina.

It is the time of the Korean War, 1951, and Casey's father David is in that war, flying planes in Asia. To stave off loneliness and to earn extra money, Casey's mother takes a second job and sends Casey off to David's parents for the summer break from school. The novel begins "Casey came unwillingly" (3). Soon after she is there she meets Dwayne, whom she had not known from earlier visits, as he had formerly lived in another part of their small town. Friendly, good-natured, harmless, though an embarrassment to his older and politically ambitious brother Alva, Dwayne passes his days playing solitaire baseball—throwing a ball at a steel drum and, depending on its bounce, giving his imagined batter a hit or an out. As if on radio, he calls his own games to an invisible audience and to any passerby like Casey: "Reese steps into the box, ready to see what Dickson will give him this time. Pee Wee's oh-for-three so far today. He's flied to left, walked, and grounded to third" (7).

Though he wants nothing to do with girls, Dwayne accepts

Casey because he mistakenly believes she is a boy and soon has her playing baseball with him. To give herself a summertime companion whom she believes she will like, Casey encourages the deception and urges her grandmother and the others in the neighborhood to go along. Soon Dwayne and Casey are fast friends, the twelve-year-old girl/boy and the retarded adult—going to movies, visiting the stores downtown, playing cards, simply enjoying each other's company.

Among their adventures is the Saturday dirt-track races where Casey's Uncle Taylor, her father's younger brother, tests his souped-up Mercury. His latest "steady girl" Gwen cheers him on, though she voices her discomfort at the constant attendance of Taylor's niece and the retarded Dwayne. Soon all realize, Jane with some motherly misgivings, that this relationship for Taylor is more serious, that indeed Gwen might be the one to catch him.

Already caught up with matrimonial plans, after a twenty-five-year courtship, are Hazard and Pansy. A bachelor, formerly a traveling salesman, Hazard regularly stays with Jane and Ben Flanagan, living there for two weeks while the restaurant in which he works as a dancing waiter is closed for summer vacation. But this summer, because of the illness of the owner, the restaurant has closed its doors permanently and Hazard has returned to Jane's house and, he hopes, to a job at Ben's lumberyard. Yet first he has to take stock of himself, of what little he has made of his life, and, worst of all, of his steadfast reluctance to admit his love for Jane's best friend Pansy and to ask her to marry him. On impulse, on Casey's first night at the Flanagan dinner table where, on Thursdays Pansy and Hazard have joined Jane and Ben for dinner since time unremembered, he proposes to Pansy. To everyone's surprise, possibly including her own, she accepts.

Their marriage a few weeks later begins well, with Casey singing at their reception and Hazard, a dancing man, hoofing for the guests. But joy soon dissolves into burlesque. For their wedding trip to Washington, D.C., Hazard forgets, first, to secure a train compartment and Pansy and he have to sit up in the parlor car. Then he leaves a bag of hers at the station and, while she awaits him in their hotel room, he goes to retrieve it. When, hours later, he has not returned, Pansy goes to the hotel lobby and sees Hazard in the bar with two acquaintances from his salesman days. His fears about their impending closeness have so frightened him that he loses track of time and, then, of Pansy. They catch the next train home and Pansy says she is through with Hazard, who returns to live at the Flanagans'. No one, not even good friend Jane, is told what went on in Washington, but Pansy has told her the marriage cannot work and she must seek an annulment. Jane recommends a cooling-off period, saying that forgiveness can come with it. Nonetheless, Pansy remains adamant in her refusal to permit Hazard into her house and back into her life.

A few weeks later, sick with the misery he caused Pansy and the subsequent sorrow that misery is causing him, Hazard attempts a counterstroke. Pansy has announced that she has seen a lawyer and Hazard responds that no divorce is possible and that, further, he will win her over even if it is his last act. Embarrassing her at her job with flowers and attention, he next pitches a tent in her front yard, but all to no avail: Pansy will have none of him.

It takes a near tragic event in Dwayne's life for Pansy to see the good in Hazard and become his wife after all. Dwayne's Saturday job is to cut the lawn at his brother Alva's house. Alva's shrewish wife Marge and Dwayne get into a heated argument about his accidentally-on-purpose mowing down her azalea plants and, in anger, Dwayne takes her car out to the dirt track. Dwayne races Marge's car around the empty track, reporting to himself that he is winning his solitary race. Casey arrives, senses the situation, and lures Dwayne off the track by announcing over the loudspeaker that he has won and must drive, slowly, into the infield to collect his trophy. Taylor has a spare one to give Dwayne. At the moment of this hoked-up presentation Alva and the sheriff arrive to arrest Dwayne for auto theft. Alva is talked out of pressing charges against his own brother, but swears that next time he will have no alternative but to put Dwayne in a home, where, indeed, Dwayne had once spent a few months and about which he still harbors a mortal dread.

That next time comes soon. Confronted by a gang of toughs at the dirt track who damage his car, Taylor gets into a fistfight and Dwayne backs him up. It is the first time he has ever hit or hurt anyone and he vomits in emotional revulsion after the fight. For Alva, this is the end and he has Dwayne committed. The sheriff comes for Dwayne at Pansy's house where he and Casey are guarding Hazard's tent so that Pansy won't take it down while he is away at work. It is the end of the day and all are there— Jane, Ben, Taylor, Pansy and Hazard, Casey and Dwayne, and a reluctant but duty-bound sheriff. Casey is enraged that no one can stop the law from taking Dwayne, first to jail for the night, then to the hospital the next morning, and all the Flanagans and Hazard and Pansy vow they will not sit idly by and see Dwayne taken from their midst. It is then that Pansy realizes how much good there really is in her hapless husband, trying though he may be: "I know you, Hazard Whitaker, and you are worth the risk" (192).

That night at a meeting of the city board, on which Alva sits, the entire Flanagan delegation presents Dwayne's case: he hurts nobody, is friendly to all (more than can be said for his older brother Alva), and is much beloved in his neighborhood, whose inhabitants will continue to care for him. With public sentiment from the mayor, the barber, the town movie owner, and everyone else who knows Dwayne arrayed against him, Alva has little choice but to relent and rescind his court order to have Dwayne committed.

The celebratory party takes its toll on Casey, who awakes from it sick, she thinks, only in her stomach. Then she realizes that she cannot move her legs. It could be polio, a disease that has ravaged much of the area in these pre-Salk days, and the family is as distraught as it is helpless. Grandmother Jane, relieved by Pansy, by Taylor, by Ben and Hazard, sits hourly with Casey, sponging her with alcohol, talking to her, reminding Casey and herself that this is the daughter she never had, telling her tales of her father when he was her age. It is during this time, too, that Dwayne learns the truth about Casey's sex. Seated on the front porch with the rest of the sorrowful family, he overhears the doctor refer to Casey as a sick little girl and he storms from the gathering.

But he is there the next day when her fever breaks and she recovers and he gives her flowers. "Girls like flowers" (221). He is there, too, when a fully recovered Casey has to return home, and it is his send-off at the bus station that means the most: "Hey, boy," he says, just as he had said it all summer (237). Looking with tear-filled eyes from her bus window at Ben and Jane, at Pansy and Hazard, at Taylor and Gwen, and especially at Dwayne who will be in their protective love and care for as long as he and they are around, Casey realizes that everything is all together now.

Bridgers set about writing this second book, concerned, as all authors must be, that the success of the first had been a fluke.[5] With *All Together Now* she demonstrated that she had many stories to tell and the skill to tell them. As the critics noted, in this work she wove several stories into one novel—Casey and Dwayne's, Pansy and Hazard's, Taylor and Gwen's, and Ben and Jane's. Writing in *Horn Book* K. M. Flanagan called the novel "exceptional not only for its superb writing and skillful portrayal of human relationships but for its depiction of a small southern town, where everyone knows everyone and neighbors care enough to rally in times of trouble."[6] *Booklist* picked up on Dwayne's baseball jargon, saying of the book: "It's a hit."[7] *Publisher's Weekly* noted the continuation of Bridgers's success with *Home before Dark*: "Proof that Bridgers's excellent novel, *Home before Dark*, was not beginner's luck is this even more memorable work. . . . Adults as well as teenagers appreciated the author's first novel and so did critics. The reaction to her second novel will surely be the same."[8]

In a most intriguing review Katherine Paterson, the deservedly acclaimed author of such novels as *Bridge to Terabithia* and *The Great Gilly Hopkins*, likened the interweaving of the four couples' stories to a square dance: "The various partners dance together and interact with the others in the square and then come home again." Jane and Ben are the head couple and the others "counter and clash" against their "solid harmony." It is, Paterson wrote, "a book for all of us who crave a good story about people we will come to care about deeply."[9]

But not all critics agreed about *All Together Now*. Although Sara Miller's review in *School Library Journal* called the book "warm and well-written," she also labeled it "overly sentimental." Miller's main objection was to the shifting points of view among the characters: "Seeing through so many eyes, readers lose Casey herself too often, and more important, lose a sense of dramatic tension."[10] Of this same shift in point of view, however, Paterson wrote of "a consciousness of a presence behind the characters— not an intrusive 19th century author-observer, to be sure—but a presence all the same." This presence is, of course, Bridgers as author-creator. About this technique Paterson continued with praise: "I hesitate to say that a writer can't change points of view so often or enter into her own story. Bridgers has, and if she has not gotten clean away with it, she has certainly written a lovely book."[11]

While the critics were being generally very favorable in their commentary about *All Together Now*, Bridgers was writing another book, one some critics found less lovely.

Notes for Another Life

Published in 1981, Bridgers's third novel, *Notes for Another Life*, again explores living in a small North Carolina town. Unlike *All Together Now*, which takes place in the 1950s, this novel is set in the present day, but the small town values remain: the importance of family, the sense of community and neighbors, the centrality of the church. Again Bridgers examines the relationship that obtains between teenagers and their grandparents; again she virtually skips a generation, just as she had in *All Together Now* with Casey's parents absent from that novel.

The novel opens with thirteen-year-old Wren Jackson and her grandmother Bliss visiting Tom, the father of Wren, the son of Bliss, at the mental institution where he has been an intermittent patient for much of his adult life and from which, though he may return home occasionally, he will probably never be completely released. His steady withdrawal from life's problems is in part a reaction to the ambition of his wife Karen, Wren's and Kevin's mother. Karen has succumbed to the lure of Atlanta, where she works as a production designer for a large department store. Kevin, Wren's sixteen-year-old brother, refuses to visit their father, resenting him for his madness and resenting their mother for her absence. Still, Wren and Bliss make the weekly trip, helping to ease their sorrow with the singing of songs; music is as central to their lives as eating. Paradoxically the Jackson family is both complete and incomplete. Grandparents Bliss and Bill and grandchildren Kevin and Wren exist in daily harmony and love, yet seldom do any of them forget the absent generation.

Although Tom is no better this week than he was last week or the week before that, the promise of new medicine offers some hope for Wren and Bliss, something they tell Karen when she makes one of her infrequent fly-in and fly-out visits to her children later that week. The news matters little to Karen; her bigger concerns are her impending promotion and transfer to Chicago and her decision to divorce Tom. Still, however, she cannot tell Kevin and Wren about the divorce; that task she leaves for her mother-in-law Bliss. The news of the move to Chicago is traumatic enough, fueling Kevin's anger and sense of despair about his parents' seeming inability to love him—the father because of mental illness, the mother because of personal goals in the business world.

He is wrong: Karen does love him, at least in her own way and from a distance. Wren understands better than Kevin her mother's drive for success, as it mirrors her own desires to become a great pianist. These are currently being confused, however, with a new and developing emotion for Wren: her sense of love. Sam Holland, bright, decent, handsome, from a solid and supportive family, a high school freshman (Wren is ending her eighth-grade year), seems to be everything a young girl could want, provided that young girl knows what she wants. Wren does not. Torn between her love of music, its career possibilities, and her intense eagerness to avoid the mistakes and unhappiness that plague her mother's life, she remains tentative about Sam's attentions. As she and Sam date more, however, Wren begins to understand that love and purpose can be entwined, that her mother's all-or-nothing choice does not have to be hers. "Loving Sam was what would make everything right. She wouldn't be like Karen, giving up husband and children for a career" (194).

Kevin's error about his mother's attitudes toward him lingers and festers. Already a loner whose only interests are tennis and girlfriend Melanie, Kevin continues to withdraw into himself, lashing out at his mother during her occasional visits, refusing to interact with his father, then guiltily hating himself for these acts of intolerance. It is he, too, who triggers his father's relapse by inadvertently mentioning the upcoming divorce. Kevin begins to doubt his own sanity: Is he like his father? His mood swings become too much for Melanie, who elects a cooling-off period in their relationship. This devastating blow to his already bruised ego couples with a broken arm—no tennis this summer—and Kevin is overwhelmed. Not long thereafter he attempts suicide.

Though Bliss discovers in time to rush him to the hospital that Kevin has swallowed a bottle of sleeping pills secreted from his grandfather's pharmacy, Kevin's destructive behavior brings to a climax the conflicting responses of the important others in his life. Through the intervention of the new minister, a man who is a bit suspect in the small community because he rides a motorcycle and seems a tad too modern, Kevin gets well and gains considerable maturity about his actions and his life. He comes to understand that Chicago and life in an apartment there with his workaholic mother is really no more desirable for him than for her. Tom's brief return home following a seemingly successful shock treatment fails after all and he must return to the hospital, this time with sympathy and the fulfilled promise of regular visits from Kevin, as well as from the faithful Wren and Bliss. Melanie, still a not-at-all-forgotten love, can remain a friend and who knows what the future might bring for them? And Bliss, already the victim of a son lost to mental illness, at least has her grandson, so like his father, returned to her.

All then ends, if not well, at least better. Wren has Sam and the beginnings of a mature relationship. Kevin knows more about himself and likes himself better. Bliss, the surrogate mother, has both Wren and Kevin, not solace completely for the lost Tom and the failed marriage between him and Karen, but comfort and challenge nonetheless. The future looks brighter.

In *Notes for Another Life* Bridgers again produced a novel acclaimed by the critics, even if a bit less enthusiastically than were her two previous efforts. The novel met with a dissenting boo here and there. Arguably, she suffered because of her previous successes: critics had come to expect too much. Robert Small, for example, in *ALAN Review* thought that the book was "flawed by a sentimental tone and characters who rarely take on the spark of life. It is not the equal of the author's fine earlier novels, *Home before Dark* and *All Together Now*."[12] The *New York Times* echoed the controversy about point of view that had surfaced in reviews of *All Together Now*: "If only she didn't jump back and forth so often from one character's viewpoint to another's! At the end the reader feels that he's been on a series of short trips rather than on a continuous journey."[13]

Writing in *School Library Journal*, Janet French attacked the book jacket blurb—"this is a family chronicle for all ages"—saying, "It would have been more accurate to describe [*Notes for Another Life*] as a propaganda vehicle for female domesticity. Good women subordinate their talents and yearnings to the home and their children; all other paths lead to havoc."[14] Her negative comments did not go unnoticed. A later issue had two letters that attacked both French and her review. Said one: "I feel that by omission your reviewer did try to make up the review user's mind and was unfair to the book." From the other: "Janet French's review of *Notes* . . . is inaccurate, unfair and uninformative. Her plot summary is flip and superficial; and her contention that the book is 'a propaganda vehicle for female domesticity' reveals (to me, anyway) that French's reading of the novel was equally flip and superficial."[15]

Had they needed them, these letter writers could have drawn on other critics who found in *Notes for Another Life* the same Bridgers whose books they had come to love. Dick Abrahamson wrote, "*Home before Dark* and *All Together Now* quickly established Bridgers's reputation in the YA field and *Notes for Another*

Life puts her at the head of the pack."[16] *Horn Book* called it "an excellent novel"[17] and *VOYA* (*Voice of Youth Advocates*) accurately labeled it a sure candidate for year-end awards.[18] Even the *New York Times* critic who described the shifting points of view as a "series of short trips" admitted that "the travel has been rewarding."[19]

At this stage in her career, then, Bridgers had written three novels, two of which (*Home before Dark* and *All Together Now*) earned exceedingly high marks from critics and teachers. Even *Notes for Another Life* had more A's than F's on its collective report card. All, however, had found their principal audiences among teenagers, young adult readers. Was Bridgers becoming pegged as a young adult author? If so, her next novel changed the image.

Sara Will

Bridgers's fourth novel, *Sara Will* (1984), was both intended for and read primarily by an adult audience. It was too slow-moving, too quiet, too lacking in any sort of major focus on an adolescent character to appeal to teenagers. Very possibly it was too long. Many young adult readers simply will not pick up any book that goes much over two hundred pages; *Sara Will* has 307. Not yet out in paperback (the reading preference of adolescents), this novel seems destined for library checkout desks, not for bookstore counter sales or classroom adoptions in school or college settings. Thus, many readers will not encounter Sara Will Burney, her sister Swanee Hope, and their "family"—Fate (short for Lafayette), his niece Eva and her out-of-wedlock baby Rachel, and Eva's suitor Michael. It is an interesting mix of characters in an interesting story.

That story opens on old-maid Sara Will and her sister Swanee Hope, both of them in their mid-fifties, who are living out their lives in the old homestead outside Tyler Mills, the house they were born and reared in. Swanee has been away, living in the nearby town, where she married and had a son who now lives in California. At the opening of the novel she is widowed and back home with Sara. It is, at best, a fragile sisterly harmony, yet one they have become accustomed to and one likely to be their lot for the rest of their lives. Swanee spends her days interacting with quiz and game shows on the television set. Sara Will devotes much of her time to tending the cemetery near their house, where all of her forebears except her sister Serena are buried.

Serena lies in a small grave on an island in the middle of a lake created by a Tennessee Valley Authority dam. Though officials had promised a road and a bridge out to that island, they had never delivered and Sara Will has not visited her sister's grave since the valley was flooded years earlier. Her letters of complaint and demand go unanswered, as if no one but she cared for the few souls buried in that small cemetery. Even Swanee is indifferent about this passion of Sara Will's. Soon, however, other concerns come into their lives, in the form of Fate, Eva, and Rachel.

Earlier, Eva became pregnant, the result of a silly moment of casual passion with a high school classmate she barely knows, and she has elected to have the baby. Her parents' outrage and the likelihood that her mother will control the rearing of her infant drive Eva away. With no other place to go, she visits seldom-seen Uncle Fate, her father's brother, a lonely, one-armed and long-since-divorced day laborer who lives some distance from her home. He takes her in, lies to her parents about his knowledge of her whereabouts, and becomes a loving surrogate parent for Eva as they await the birth of her child, an event that gives Fate a purpose in life—he must protect Eva and Rachel.

The first step in this protection involves getting her somewhere where her parents cannot find her. He decides on Sara Will's house, a place he has visited once, years before, at Serena's funeral. He recalls the isolation of that homeplace now and heads there.

Little could be more disruptive to Sara Will's severely ordered existence than the intrusion of Fate, Eva, and baby Rachel. Though Swanee Hope carries on with overmuch sentiment (to Sara's way of thinking), Sara herself grudgingly allows the newcomers only a few days in this sanctuary. Then they must move on. But before they go, Michael arrives. He is not Rachel's father, yet he is desperately in love with Eva and eager to marry her, a love not at all reciprocated. He soon is equally in love with baby Rachel.

Despite Sara Will's minimal hospitality (compensated for by Swanee Hope's excessive generosity), days pile upon days and soon new agreements are reached: Fate, Eva, Rachel, and Michael can stay until Christmas. There will even be a Christmas party, the first time the Burney house has had such an affair since before the death of Serena decades earlier. During the preparations Sara begins to see much that is good in Fate, just as he senses himself falling in love with her. But it is easier for him, Sara knows. He has been married before. He has not been strong, as she has, not carried the burden of a restricted life as she has, not been so wedded to old ways that change of any kind is difficult and marriage is almost beyond contemplation. She was "frightened, forever watchful, unsure and questioning. What is the right thing to do? she would ask herself, never willing to concede the possibility of several solutions" (269).

Sara is wrong about Fate. He, too, is troubled by these new feelings of love. Still, he does make the first move. On Christmas Day he brings an early morning cup of coffee to Sara in her sparsely furnished bedroom, about which he remarks astutely: "Why, there's nothing of you in here. Where do you keep yourself, Sara?" And then he plunges ahead with what he has long wanted to say, his kind of proposal: "I just know that I have feelings for you that can probably stay just like they are, hidden and small because I'm good at that. Or they can grow. . . . If you're willing, Sara, what I feel for you will grow" (182).

Sara is willing and plans are made for a spring wedding, something she had convinced herself would never happen to her. In the meantime Michael's importunings to Eva have had some effect, particularly his telling her that he has proposed for the last time. She is likely to accept. Eva's parents come to the Burney house, having found Eva through a letter Michael had written to his parents telling where he was. They are furious with Fate because of his duplicity, but more forgiving about Eva, who decides to remain on at Sara's as planned until Rachel's birthday. Then she will decide what to do about Michael and about her parents. Too, she can stay for the wedding of Sara Will and Fate, if ever there is to be a wedding.

It is not that Sara Will does not love Fate; it is rather that she cannot be certain that marriage and its altered life-style are for her. Second thoughts cause her almost to break the engagement when Fate has an accident with her beloved Mustang. She leaves the house and goes to a boardinghouse in nearby Tyler Mills. Dejected, she stays there only a few days and returns home, sure now that she does in fact want to marry Fate.

A short time later they do marry. At their wedding Eva confesses her own love for Michael, saying that she will return to her parents' home that summer and that she and Michael will see each other. And Swanee plans first a trip to California to see her son and grandchildren and then a return to her home in Tyler Mills, leaving the Burney house for Fate and Sara. The concluding pages of the novel describe the trip all of them take to the island where Serena is buried, traveling on a boat Fate has purchased and rebuilt. It is a fitting climax: Through her death years earlier Serena had brought them all together.

Though authors often say that asking them to choose their favorites among their novels is like asking them to choose their favorites among their children, Sue Ellen Bridgers is quick to respond, when queried about her favorite character, that it is Sara Will. Many of the critics shared her love for this character and for the novel that bears her name.

For the *Charlotte Observer* Dannye Romine observed: "In Sue Ellen Bridgers's meticulously controlled hands this novel unfolds and blossoms slowly, quietly, almost rhythmically. Nothing knocks you down or pulls you under water. Instead, Bridgers offers the quiet, sure drama of love being born, of hearts softening, of emotions picking up the beat of life."[20] Calling the novel a "quietly moving book of affirming love," *Library Journal* reviewer Jeanne Buckley no doubt particularly endeared herself to Bridgers; she began her review with a comparison of Bridgers's work with that of Anne Tyler, Bridgers's favorite novelist.[21] Mary K. Chelton called it "Bridgers's finest novel."[22]

Yet Chelton, as did other reviewers and certainly many readers, cautioned that it was not a young adult book: "This novel cannot in any way be construed as YA. It is an *adult* love story."[23] *Washington Post* reviewer Alice Digilio ended her essentially negative judgments with her "hope that Bridgers return to her old metier—novels for adolescents that speak more honestly, that tell more authentic stories." Digilio had earlier noted that this book represented Bridgers's first attempt at a novel intended primarily for an adult audience and had accused her of slipping beyond sentiment to sentimentality, though she grudgingly admitted Bridgers's "brilliance with words."[24] The direction seemed plain: Bridgers should return home before dark, home to adolescent literature. She did.

Permanent Connections

In *Permanent Connections*, published in 1987, Bridgers revisits a story line explored in *All Together Now*: the youngster separated from his or her parents and placed in a rural environment among older relatives. Unlike Casey of the earlier book, however, seventeen-year-old Rob Dickson barely knows his grandfather, his Uncle Fairlee, and Aunt Coralee, and what he does know of them, he does not like. They live in small-town North Carolina, not even in the village but on a small farm a few miles from town, as unlike his native New Jersey, Rob thinks, as the earth from the moon. And yet there he is stuck, at least for a while.

At odds with his parents because he seems purposeless and drifting, frequently drunk, high on occasional pot, often at odds, too, with himself, Rob does not want to accompany his father, Davis, when they must return to the homeplace to look after Uncle Fairlee, who has broken his hip. Fairlee keeps house, in effect, for his aged father, Rob's grandfather, and for his sister, Rob's Aunt Coralee, who is an agoraphobe, unwilling even to venture from the safety of their house to her own back porch. Though able to afford a housekeeper to care for the trio, Davis cannot find one and prevails upon a most reluctant Rob to remain from late summer to December to help out. Rob will lift the still-crippled Fairlee out of bed, do the shopping, and generally be the physical strength and the outside presence the three older people need. It is, Rob knows, a dismal prospect, made only a little more palatable by Davis's promise to ship Rob his portable tv and his stereo and records.

Near the Dickson homestead is the mountain home of Ginny Collier, which she built for herself and her teenage daughter Ellery after her divorce from Ellery's father and their departure from urban Charlotte. Ellery hates the rural life as intensely as Rob. When the two meet and then date, their unhappiness with their lives soon spreads to a kind of love-hate, on-again/off-again relationship. Though she could return to Charlotte and live with her father, Ellery must grudgingly admit that she would be in his way and is better off in Tyler Mills.

Rob and Ellery sometimes double-date with Leanna and her lifetime steady, Travis Williams. While Travis himself does not use marijuana, his older brothers raise it in abundance hidden in the mountains behind their home, something Travis tells the worldly Rob. At a time when he is discouraged with life—he and Ellery have fought again, school in this backwoods town seems no better than the one he had left in New Jersey, his grandpa and Aunt Coralee don't take to his "modern" ways—Rob begs two marijuana cigarettes from a hesitant Travis. In a pot-induced stupor exacerbated by bad road conditions and pouring rain, Rob drives Uncle Fairlee's truck into a ditch. He leaves the truck to get help, then decides to wait by it until someone comes along, but when he returns, a patrolman is on the scene and, having found the two roaches on the truck seat, arrests Rob for possession. Ginny Collier pays his bail so that he can be released from jail pending trial.

During these first two months of Rob's stay Ginny has been working with Coralee on their mutual love of sewing and, using that shared interest, trying to draw Coralee out of her fearful shell. Her efforts succeed, a little. Initially Coralee will go out on the porch of her home, the first time in several years she has left her house. Next she ventures into the yard, but only with Ginny there for physical and psychological support.

While they await his trial, relations between Ellery and Rob deteriorate almost beyond repair. They have had one sexual encounter and, though each feels in love with the other, they still cannot be together without fighting. In fact, Rob's relationships with almost everyone are shattered by his surliness and selfishness and his vacillating feelings about Ellery. He argues, mopes, feels sorry for himself. Uncle Fairlee's patient wisdom helps Rob see what he is doing not only to himself but also to others. Yet it takes an accident to his grandfather to make Rob really envision a different and perhaps better future for himself.

After a bitter argument which he has caused, Rob rushes from the Dickson house into the storm-filled night and, later, falls asleep in Fairlee's truck in the lot of a country church where he and Ellery had once parked. Returning home well after midnight, he finds Fairlee and Coralee in a frenzied turmoil. His infirm grandfather has gone after Rob, on foot, and has been gone for hours. Possibly he is dead. The mentally damaged Coralee, who is improved but still unable to leave the security of her yard, and the physically crippled Fairlee cannot go out into the night to find him. Realizing that it was he who caused the old man to leave the house, Rob begins the search and finds his grandfather nearly unconscious on the bank of a creek, where he had slipped and fallen. He gets grandpa back home and then to the hospital, accompanied by Coralee, who forgets her own fears in anxiety about her father.

Grandpa has broken ribs and a punctured lung, but he will live. Through the old man's spirit Rob learns something about courage and about himself. His self-awareness grows through the aid of a priest he meets in the little country church where he has gone to try to pray. Rob's father, Davis, returns for the drug trial and he and a newly mature Rob strike a warmer chord than has existed between them for years. Says Davis of the trial: "You'll have to take what's coming to you without complaint. . . . But I'll be there with you" (237).

And almost everyone else important to Rob is there, too. Still shy, still uncertain, but clearly on the road to normalcy, Coralee is in the courtroom, with instructions to call Fairlee as soon as the trial ends. Leanna and Travis provide support, the latter no longer worried that Rob might tell where he got the marijuana. Most important to Rob, Ginny and Ellery are there. It is clear that Rob has more friends than he thought he would have. He knows that in the future he must work to deserve their trust.

As it happens, the trial is brief. Able to point out that Rob was not actually in the truck when the officer discovered it and that, therefore, links between him and the pot were circumstantial, Rob's skillful lawyer gets the case dismissed. Rob does receive a stern lecture from the judge. It is one he will heed.

And it is one he thinks about during a mountain jog over the trails that he and Ellery had run. Will he remain here, staying near Ellery? Will he perhaps go out for the school basketball team, an action that had been beneath him in his pseudosophisticated life in New Jersey? Will he stay with Aunt Coralee and Uncle Fairlee? They are, after all, his roots, his permanent connections. The future, whatever he decides, seems bright; he has taken charge of his own life.

Any critics or readers Bridgers may have disappointed with her clearly adult novel *Sara Will* quickly returned to the fold upon encountering *Permanent Connections*. *School Library Journal* summarized her descriptions in this book with one word: "Masterful."[25] An *ALAN Review* notice began: "Sue Ellen Bridgers has done it again, written a fine, complexly textured novel about life in rural Appalachia."[26] The *English Journal* also placed the novel in the context of her earlier work: "Sue Ellen Bridgers succeeds with another beautifully written work."[27] An interesting metaphor for not only this novel but for all of Bridgers's stories was supplied in a review in the *Bulletin of the Center for Children's Books*: "Low key, small scale, this [*Permanent Connections*] has the rich intricacy of a Persian rug."[28]

About the only negative remarks concerning *Permanent Connections* focused on Rob's conversation with Tom Fowler, the sensitive and wise priest Rob meets in the small country church. He had not intended to see Fowler; Rob knows of the church because he and Ellery had parked there. But some reviewers labeled this episode "intrusive,"[29] "superfluous,"[30] and "strained,"[31] adjectives that may be too harsh. After all, the meeting between Rob and Fowler is an easily believed coincidence. And what he says to Rob—in effect, you must decide your own paths in life—is about what one would expect any minister to say to any obviously troubled teen. Bridgers says of the criticism of the role of the priest that readers who believed that Rob's meeting with him provided too easy a solution "don't know anything about the spirit. That one little conversation helped him this one time to pray, but the struggle Rob is going to have is ongoing."[32]

Critics and novelists at best have an uneasy dependency. Without the novels critics would have nothing to write about; without the reviews novelists would have a difficult time getting their works announced to a broad public. Bridgers is aware of this symbiosis and more tolerant than many about it. Not for her the overstated alliteration of Sir Thomas Beecham, who called critics "drooling, driveling, doleful, depressing, dropsical drips." Or of Charles Lamb, who said, "For critics I care the five hundred thousandth part of the tythe of a half-farthing." Though she "can hardly stand to read them,"[33] Bridgers does study what her critics have to say. She may, however, be too hard on herself, selecting out the negative sentence from among the positive paragraphs and concentrating overmuch on it, as she has in her reaction to the comments about the priest in *Permanent Connections*.

She notices, too, those reviewers who accuse her of verging on sentimentality: "I have these predisposed things that I have learned from the critics—that I have to be very careful not to be sentimental. They say I come close and that makes me know there's an edge."[34] Yet those reviewers who have commented on "the edge of sentimentality" are few, and even in their notices this criticism is never the entire substance of their judgments.

Novelist Rita Mae Brown said, "If critics want to help me, let them come sit next to me while I'm writing." Bridgers feels much the same way: Critics "can't change what I've already done. It's already done. Maybe reviews should come out when you've done your rough draft. Every book is a whole new thing and while I guess we do learn something from the last book it's hard to see how I make what I learned work in another one."[35] Obviously, though, Bridgers has learned: her stories, her characters, her themes, her use of setting, her writing style all attest to that.

3. A Creator of Characters

It is a difficult question for writers: which comes first, the characters or the plot? Different authors vary in their responses. W. Somerset Maugham says, "You can never know enough about your characters." Other writers talk of how their characters take over their stories. Playwright Luigi Pirandello puts it this way: "When the characters are really alive before their author, the latter does nothing but follow them in their actions, in their words, in the situations which they suggest to him." Truman Capote goes even further: "You can't blame a writer for what the characters say."

Wrong, say such novelists as Vladimir Nabokov and John Cheever. Nabokov: "That trite little whimsy about characters getting out of hand; it is as old as the quills. My characters are galley slaves." And Cheever: "The legend that characters run away from their author—taking up drugs, having sex operations, becoming president—implies that the writer is a fool with no knowledge or mastery of his craft. The idea of authors running around helplessly behind their cretinous inventions is contemptible."

Sue Ellen Bridgers is in the former camp. She begins her novels with a concentration on her characters, more precisely a single character—a Sara Will or a Rob Dickson around whom she will build her story. "When I'm writing fiction, what I think has to be secondary. What the character feels and does is primary," she says.[1] In another speech she argues, "Some writers would say the plot is the way to fiction's wisdom and I would not disagree completely. . . . But I would rather recommend the character, the person inside the event. I would give you a spirit clothed in flesh and blood and then I would select out of all the possibilities of time and place, a situation where that person could be most fully revealed."[2] Another of her statements addresses this same issue: "Technically the characters always come first and then the kind of people they are dictates what they do."[3]

During the three years it takes Bridgers to produce a novel it is in the first year, the time when she is getting to know her characters, that the juices must really flow. Then the migrant family seen in the station wagon can become the Willis family of *Home before Dark*. Dwayne, first described to Bridgers by her husband, who had known a Dwayne type in a small town he once lived in, can begin the solitary baseball games that he enjoys in *All Together Now*. As she puts it, "I don't approach the typewriter until the characters are fully revealed to me, until I feel comfortable with their ability to tell me their story and my ability to be receptive to it."[4]

She tells how she met the other major figures in her novels in one of her speeches:

> I wrote the first lines of *Notes for Another Life* on a Hallmark pocket calendar because I was driving the car at the time. At that moment I felt Bliss and Wren's presence with me and knew their inherent sadness. I heard their brave singing. One day a few years ago I saw Sara Will Burney coming down the road in the twilight. I wrote down exactly what I saw and so a person was born out of my imagination onto the page. The first time I saw Rob Dickson, the protagonist of *Permanent Connections*, he was sulking. His eyes held that hooded look that defies investigation. His face was tight and bitter but over a period of months he did reveal himself to me. We had a hard time of it but finally I knew him well enough to commit my understanding to paper.[5]

To Bridgers "what the character feels and does is primary." In that principle may well lie one explanation of why her characters are so memorable: their creator is interested in them. "My characters are more crucial than any other element in my approach to the writing of fiction."[6] It is thus appropriate to study Bridgers's novels and stories with a focus on her characters.

The Adolescents in Bridgers's Works

Above all else, a novelist who wants adolescent readers must create significant adolescent characters, the kinds of people other teenagers will want to read about, think about, share joy and misery with, come to recognize as peers. Bridgers has created just such people, beginning with her first adolescent, Stella Willis in *Home before Dark*.

Stella is initially seen as the Willis family is approaching the old Willis homestead that James Earl had left years earlier. Those years of living in the station wagon or in grimy housing at the edge of the fields they worked, being in and out of school, not always getting medical attention, have taken their toll on Stella: "At fourteen she was thin and fair, with the dingy, fading pallor of intermittent sunburns to her skin. She looked like a discarded doll, with dry fiber hair" (4). Though Stella may seem discarded, she is not defeated. Her Aunt Anne recognizes her "spark" on their first meeting and soon Stella is seen as determined to confront her new life on its own terms, without Mae's weak-kneed intervention: "She can't hold me back anymore, Stella thought" (117).

Soon Stella gets to know the smitten Rodney Biggers, but maturely realizes how devious he really is. After he has arranged to have Toby beaten by thugs, Stella confronts Rodney with her final words: "You're gonna look like a skunk, Rodney, because what you did to Toby is so stinking and hateful and yellow that I'll remember it every time I look at you" (135).

Other crises reveal Stella's extraordinary strength. When her mother Mae dies, it is Stella who assumes an adult role: "I'm going to the house to see about Daddy. He needs me now" (91). After James Earl's decision to marry Maggie Grover and move from the tenant shack into town, Stella refuses to join him and the rest of the family. It is not that she dislikes Maggie. Rather, she loves the land, her land after all, too, and cannot leave it. Yet, in the end, a wiser and more mature Stella does come to town to live, a young woman able to understand that "I can leave my little house and not be giving it up, because what I feel about it will come with me" (173).

Reviewers were quick to see in the creation of Stella a character worthy of high commendations. Two comments exemplify the general sense of them all. Said the *Women in Libraries Newsletter*: "Stella's coming of age is done superbly."[7] And Betsy Lindau wrote in the *Southern Pines Pilot*: "Stella has what it takes to make it. She is an absolutely unique person it will be hard for you to forget—and her story as told by Sue Ellen Bridgers will ring true to anyone who has found themselves lost at sea—or on dry land. Know Stella and take heart!"[8]

Equal praise followed the portrait of Casey, the adolescent whose story frames Bridgers's next novel, *All Together Now*. The *Charlotte Observer* yearned that fiction would become fact: "It would be nice to believe that people like Casey Flanagan and her friends do exist. And if they don't, they should!"[9] Though strong, Casey is no Stella, faced with the having-to-grow-up-in-a-hurry life of the migrant worker child. Casey can afford to be dependent: on her parents (despite their absence from the story), her grandparents, even friends like Dwayne and Hazard and Pansy.

In most novels intended for young adult audiences an adolescent serves as the centerpiece, around whom the rest of the characters revolve and the plot lines are developed. Not so with *All Together Now*, despite the fact that the beginning and end—two significant parts of any novel—focus primarily on Casey Flanagan. The rest is as much Dwayne's story as Casey's. It is also, and importantly, the story of Pansy and Hazard, Gwen and Taylor, and, indeed, the entire town. Yet Casey merits the attention critics and readers have given her.

The opening sentence refers to Casey's reluctance about spending the entire summer with her grandparents in their tiny community far from her home city. But she stays on, to earn and give love, and to board the bus late in August for mother and home a very different youngster from the one who arrived two months earlier. Her first encounter is with Dwayne, whom she deceives so that he will let her join in his baseball game. "She had never lied, at least not a big lie, a gigantic lie, one that could change her summer. Yet the proportions of her dishonesty didn't scare her, for it seemed right, both for her and for Dwayne Pickens, that she should say the words that would give them both so much pleasure" (18). So she let him believe she was a boy and it was "Batter up!"

Casey's trials, the struggles that Bridgers wants all her major characters to be engaged in, come later in the novel. First Casey helps Hazard rectify the tragicomedy he has made of his and Pansy's honeymoon. Only then does she take on the moral center of the novel. When Dwayne is to be institutionalized, everyone has failed him, she thinks, but she most of all. Taylor's persuasion at the town council meeting restores Dwayne to his home and Casey to her earlier more intelligent view of the decency of adults.

Then serious illness strikes Casey, giving her another test. Her own strength meshes with the physical and prayerful support of virtually the entire community and Casey recovers, but as a different child. She is still in her grandmother's house, in the room her father had used as a child, yet changed nonetheless. She is now closer to her family, her father in Korea, her mother on the other side of North Carolina, Jane and Ben, Pansy and Hazard, Taylor and Gwen, and, most of all, Dwayne. She is all together now.

Next in Bridgers's line of adolescent characters came a brother and sister, Wren and Kevin in *Notes for Another Life*. As in *All Together Now*, Bridgers virtually skips a generation. Casey spent a summer with her paternal grandparents. Wren and Kevin have spent most of their lives with their grandparents, Bliss and Ben. With their father in a mental institution, their mother in Atlanta, Wren and Kevin are really more the children of Bliss and Bill than of Tom and Karen.

The shift in parentage is harder on Kevin. Though he loves and has sympathy for his father, he is emotionally unprepared to make the visits to him that Bliss and Wren courageously undergo every Saturday. He confuses his mother's out-of-town business ventures with rejection of him and Wren, especially him. A broken arm ends his summer tennis, his strangeness causes girlfriend Melanie to suggest they part for at least a while, and he constantly worries that the mental illness of his father will be visited upon him. He even so describes himself to Melanie. "You think I'm sick, don't you? You think there's something wrong with me. Well, maybe there is. I feel crazy. That's the truth. Maybe I am" (170).

Tom is, of course, patterned at least somewhat after Bridgers's own father, who from time to time during her youth was institutionalized with depression that occasionally developed into catatonia. And she admits that Kevin and Wren, particularly the former, mirror feelings she and her sister had when they were growing up—anger at what not having a "normal" father sometimes cost them, self-pity, fears that they were in some ways responsible for his condition and that they themselves might suffer from it in their own adult lives.[10] *Notes for Another Life* is far from autobiography, but it touches more closely on Bridgers's early years than do any of her other novels. She writes about Kevin with extraordinary insight.

Unlike Bridgers herself, however, who had the most supportive of mothers, Kevin has a mother who he thinks has chosen not to be with him. At great cost he tells her that he wants to come to Chicago with her. It is a pivotal scene:

> She had how long, five seconds? How long did it take to say yes? He would give her that long. Time to envision him in the roomy apartment, high up and with a view. Time even to put out her arms to him. He watched her fingers tightening on the edge of the magazine. She gripped it as if she were about to swat an insect, eliminate some pesky interference. Still, he waited.
>
> Time ran slowly, running out. He looked at her, eyes tearing. His vision was curiously blurred at the edges, but her face was clear to him, as solid and contained as marble.

"All right," she said, but it was too late. She had hesitated. (178)

Kevin's suicide attempt follows shortly thereafter. With the help of a minister Kevin comes to understand both himself and his mother better, and the book ends with reason for optimism for him. Though Bridgers seldom reveals too much at the end of her novels, saying "ending books is so hard, not saying too much, not ending with some kind of little thing that invalidates all of the struggles people have had,"[11] there is evidence enough to have high hopes for Kevin.

Less compellingly drawn is Kevin's thirteen-year-old sister Wren, who is much more Bliss's child and thus better able to ward off any feelings of rejection from her mother's infrequent visits or divorce and moving plans. Between her and grandmother Bliss are years of harmony that have contributed to her evenness. And Wren has her piano music, which provides her solace and sustenance. Yet Wren seems a too thoughtful, too competent little adult, more mature for her age than she ought to be. She and Sam, her first boyfriend, have rather more serious conversations than those of most eighth and ninth graders. The distant future—college, adult lives—tends to loom large in their thinking, too large.

Critics who carped that *Notes for Another Life* is sentimental may have had Wren and Sam in mind. They are Bridgers's least-realized teenagers, ironically found in a novel with Kevin, who, with Rob Dickson of *Permanent Connections*, is among her best-drawn adolescent characters.

Author, readers, critics all agree that *Sara Will* is not a young adult novel and, thus, its two adolescent characters, Eva and Michael, may be judged by standards different from those used with Stella, Casey, Wren, and Kevin. Eva and Michael are not the central characters of this novel about a woman in her mid-fifties, but minor figures. Neither Michael nor Eva conveys the sense of realism that surrounds the major figures of the novel, Sara Will and Fate, or even Swanee Hope. Both seem more victims than shapers of events, at least for most of the novel. In her one sexual encounter Eva becomes pregnant, with no love for the baby's father and few plans for its birth and future. She goes to Fate for help and follows along with his quest for protection to Sara Will's house, where she finally asserts herself a bit and asks to stay until baby Rachel's first birthday. When her parents come to visit on Christmas Day, a scene that fails to reach the high drama it might have had, Eva does summon enough gumption to tell her mother that neither the adoption nor the abortion her parents had recommended was for her; she wanted Rachel. But these instances of maturity are lost among the more common episodes of a hazy and diffident personality.

Equally adrift and with an added healthy dollop of self-pity is Michael, who, though he has never had an official date with Eva, nonetheless loves her intensely enough to follow her across North Carolina to Tyler Mills, insert himself into Sara Will's tightly run household, propose marriage to Eva and endure her frequent and angry refusals, and even fantasize that he is indeed the father of Rachel: "In his mind, his heart, in every way that could matter, Rachel was his. Given a chance, she would grow up calling him Daddy. She would get her allowance from him and a kiss good night and a story, and in the mornings he could awaken her by touching her hair so gently it would be like a moth brushing her cheek" (156). It is not easy to reconcile the thoughtfulness of Michael's imagined parental role with his rather naive behavior and lack of self-knowledge in most of the book. His and Eva's relationship borders on soap opera, a criticism that cannot be justifiably leveled at any other characters or episodes in Bridgers's writing. But Michael and Eva are not up to standard.

Rob Dickson is. In *Permanent Connections* Bridgers returns to what seems likely to be her best literary base, novels for young adults, and creates compellingly drawn teenagers, notably Rob and his friend Ellery. Again the outsider motif appears. Both Rob and Ellery are in Tyler Mills—yes, it is the same city Sara Will lives near—and both are there unhappily, against their wills. Rob must replace his injured Uncle Fairlee as the helpmate for his agoraphobic Aunt Coralee and nearly senile grandfather. Ellery lives with her mother Ginny, who has divorced her father and left Charlotte. It is to Bridgers's considerable credit that she moves her novel beyond the pseudosophisticated put-downs of Tyler Mills that Rob and Ellery share at the beginning of their friendship and goes on to explore not only their relationship but the lives of other characters as well, particularly Ginny and Cora-lee.

Yet Rob, the adolescent, remains at the center of the novel. Typically in young adult novels the adolescent protagonist, if male, is more good than bad, more noble than not, more active than passive. Rob, at the outset of the novel, is none of these. He drifts in school, smokes, drinks, is irresponsible, unlikable. Life in Tyler Mills changes him, though perhaps not fully. Again Bridgers refuses to wrap everything up neatly at the end of the novel. Still it is easy to believe that Rob will indeed remain in Tyler Mills with his extended family and to be confident about his future. His quickly formed and supercilious opinions have given way to an admiring sense of courage at Coralee's overcoming her agoraphobia, his grandfather's intense will, his uncle's good common sense, Ginny's compassion for others, Ellery's love. He has become a mature young man.

Ellery is equally well drawn, complex, full of the uncertainties most adolescents face. These are exacerbated by her move from Charlotte to Tyler Mills, by her parents' divorce, and by her developing interest in Rob, which she at first resists, telling herself: "Go away, Rob Dickson. . . . I've got all the hurt I can handle" (67). Later, she sees Rob's worth, defending him against her mother's cautious rejection, consoling him when he faces the drug use charge. For them both, life together and in Tyler Mills seems likely to be better in their future than in their past.

Stella, Casey, Kevin, Rob, and Ellery are very different adolescents, to be sure, but they share one trait: they are realistic. Complex, rounded, sometimes in control but sometimes dependent on others, they are typical teens and, because they are, they are outstanding teenage characters in the world of fiction for young adults. Less well drawn are Wren, Eva, and Michael, but the occasional flashes of brilliance that surround even their creation add to the belief that Bridgers knows her craft well in deciding to begin her stories with a clear vision of her adolescent characters. Unlike some writers of fiction for young readers, however, she is not limited in her casting, creating only interesting teens. Her other characters merit attention, too.

Bridgers's Older Women

Two generalizations may be safely made about Sue Ellen Bridgers's novels that have teenagers as central characters: the parents of the teens are weak or nonexistent and the powerful shapers of the teenagers are older women. The briefest of recapitulations supports the first of these assertions: In *Home before Dark* Stella's parents, James Earl and Mae Willis, have drifted throughout their adult lives, traveling from one migrant camp to another, rootless, with little past and less future. Not until James Earl decides to return to the homestead in North Carolina does there seem much chance for Stella to have a normal life. Even at this time Mae hopes the stay will be short, a brief visit, and it probably would have been had it not been for the kindness of Newton and Anne Willis and Stella's determination never to leave the land. Never at ease, Mae withdraws, and her sudden death ends what otherwise would probably have been an unpleasant wasting away. After Mae's death Stella takes charge of her own life.

In *All Together Now* the absence of Casey's parents is literal: her father is flying airplanes in Korea. Because her mother works two jobs, she sends Casey to her husband's hometown for the summer. They are so far out of the story that, when Casey falls ill with what all fear is polio, grandmother Jane does not even try hard to contact her daughter-in-law.

Notes for Another Life continues the pattern. Wren and Kevin have lived with their grandparents for six years. It is a good relationship, a loving one, but it is not with their parents. Tom's mental incapacity and Karen's choice of working in Atlanta permit only occasional involvement in their children's lives. Tom comes home sometimes. Karen visits between assignments. Their inconsistent participation raises, then dashes, hopes, and may even be more counterproductive than would complete absence.

Rob Dickson's story in *Permanent Connections* opens with his overhearing his parents' troubled conversation about what to do with him. This scene is virtually the last time his mother appears in the book. His father forces Rob to remain in Tyler Mills to care for the Dickson family elders and then disappears, to return briefly at Rob's trial. Like Stella, Casey, Wren, and Kevin, Rob is not getting any help from his parents. Ellery Collier, the other significant teenager in *Permanent Connections*, does live with her divorced mother Ginny, a well-drawn parental figure and a powerful character in that novel, but her presence is an exception to the rule.

Even in the adult novel *Sara Will* teenage Eva has run away from her parents to have her illegitimate child somewhere else. And Michael runs away to stay with Eva, leaving parents who barely rate a mention or a thought.

Bridgers offers some explanation for this generational gap: "I grew up in a little town with an extended family, a lot of people to feel close to, and that fact that there were other people, other than my parents, that I could turn to, obviously plays into my writing. But the fact that I have these absent parents in my novels worries me some."[12] Particularly troublesome is the absence of mothers: "I really haven't written about women who are good or even adequate mothers—in fact, I hardly write about mothers at all."[13] (Bridgers made this remark before she had written *Permanent Connections*, in which Ginny is surely an adequate mother by even the most exacting of standards.) Yet she does not want this absence in her prose misconstrued as evidence that her own relationship with her mother was an unhappy one; it was not. It was and still is warm, supportive, loving. Rather, having a geographically or emotionally distant mother provides a powerful opportunity for plot development. As she writes in that same early article, "My mothers are absent because for me, motherlessness provides the ultimate, the all-consuming conflict. No matter what the relationship is, close or distant, strained or loving, mothers are still our source. They are perhaps the most unique and certainly the most complex attachment we will ever have."[14]

Possibly. On the other hand, Bridgers may simply be finding a justification for herself for these absent mothers. For it must be said that, save for Kevin and Wren in *Notes for Another Life*, most of her adolescent protagonists worry about their mothers rather little. Stella recovers from Mae's tragic death in *Home before Dark* almost before the poor woman is buried. It is true that Casey thinks some about her mother in *All Together Now*, but not as the "complex attachment" Bridgers thinks of; Casey's more serious reflections center on her father. In *Sara Will* Eva's mother resembles a past and shadowy evil from whose wrong advice and persecution Eva must escape. Michael's mother rates but one line in a novel of several hundred pages. Possibly most notable, Rob Dickson's mother in *Permanent Connections* is hardly a connection at all, merely a worried presence early in the novel, an occasional fleeting thought elsewhere in it. In that same novel Ellery and her mother Ginny do have a complicated love-hate relationship, a beautifully described one, but Ginny is *there*, on the scene, not absent like Bridgers's other mothers.

The question, then, may be whether it is sensibility or rhetorical convenience that causes Bridgers to remove her fictional mothers from their expected roles. To further her point, Bridgers claims that placing these teenagers largely on their own both reveals more of their character and forces them to struggle with who they are and what they can do. "My own justification for absent parents in my early books [and repeated in the later novels like *Sara Will* and *Permanent Connections*] is that it makes the young persons' dilemmas, decisions, and resolutions all the more difficult and poignant."[15] Typically, they are helped in their struggles by an older person, usually a woman. In her creation of a number of memorable older women Bridgers admits to recollections of her own grandmothers in the small town where she was reared and of her continuing love and admiration for her own mother.

In *Home before Dark* Maggie Grover begins Bridgers's parade of older women who prove instrumental in the lives of the teenagers in their care. Maggie enters late in the novel, after Mae's death, and sets her sights on James Earl. She has, she knows, "a great deal to offer a man like him—money, a house and business, the mothering of his children, comfort in his loneliness, a body eager to be given" (112). James Earl quickly and eagerly accepts this offer, but Stella holds back; she does not want to move to Maggie's house with her father and her siblings. It is a wise and patient Maggie who waits for Stella, who does not force her to make a final decision. To Stella's uncertainty about whether to stay on the Willis farm or move into town to Maggie's, her new stepmother replies simply, "I can love you, Stella" (174). Soon, thereafter, Stella comes home.

Jane Flanagan plays a large role in her granddaughter Casey's life in Bridgers's next novel, *All Together Now,* and indeed in the life of the entire community. Jane does not face the getting-acquainted problems that confront Maggie Grover; she has continuing contact with Casey, from her complicity in the lie to Dwayne about Casey's gender to her round-the-clock watchfulness when Casey is ill. Jane assumes the role of mother as moral guide, commenting on Casey's failure to correct Dwayne's misapprehension that she is a boy: "Not telling him is the same as lying, Casey" (20). And later, when Dwayne is taken away, it is Jane who is wise enough to wait for a better moment to console the crestfallen and unforgiving Casey: "Jane held her, unable to say that age had taught her that people do forgive, even forget, the wrongs they've done" (197).

But Jane's role in *All Together Now* goes well beyond Casey. She joins the community effort to keep Dwayne at home. At the town council confrontation Alva appeals to Jane to agree with him about the need to put Dwayne back into a mental hospital:

"Mrs. Flanagan, you understand, don't you? You know how Mama takes care of him. What's going to happen when she is gone? Who's going to be responsible, then?"
"I don't know, Alva," Jane Flanagan said. . . . "But why make him start living such a sad life before he has to? It'll come soon enough. He's a happy person, Alva. Let him have that much now, no matter what there is to come." (204)

Jane's best friend Pansy, herself an adroitly drawn older woman, marries Hazard Whitaker, the result of his finally asking her after a courtship of some twenty-five years. Combining forgetfulness about the details of their honeymoon, a surprising insensitivity to Pansy's needs, and his own insecurity in their marriage, Hazard makes a botch of things, and Pansy decides on an annulment. It is Jane who urges patience and caution: "Whatever Hazard did, it wasn't immoral and it wasn't against the law. That means it's something you can forgive. After all, he's your husband" (132).

Notes for Another Life introduces another older woman into Bridgers's dramatis personae, Bliss Jackson, the grandmother of Kevin and Wren. Like Jane Flanagan, Bliss recognizes the difficulty of the surrogate's role, yet knows it is one from which she cannot escape, even if that were her wish, and it is not. It is an important role in the lives of both her grandchildren. With Wren she has a particularly close relationship, born partly of their shared interest in the piano—Bliss has taught Wren and encouraged her talent—and their weekly visits to see Wren's father, Tom. Bliss finds Kevin in time to thwart his suicide attempt and urges him to spend time with the Reverend Kensley, who helps Kevin to understand himself and what he did. She ultimately gets Kevin back on his beloved tennis court and adds to his recovery.

A troubled conversation between Bliss and her husband Bill offers a commentary on marriage. Bridgers seems on Bliss's side. Karen has announced in a letter that she wants a divorce from Tom, and Bliss is bitter. She echoes the better or worse, sickness and health phrases from the standard marriage vows and implies that Karen should have stuck with Tom. Yet she is uncertain. She has to be. The relationship between Tom and Karen is complex, difficult, a wonderfully drawn example of a marriage that went sour through no one's real fault. Bill is inclined to believe that a divorce may be for the best.

A few minutes later, Bliss and Bill go to bed, still unsettled by the news from Karen. Unlike their son's, their own marriage offers a safe haven in times of distress: " 'I love you, Bliss,' a voice said in the dark. Then a cool foot rested against hers and there was no accounting for the joy of it" (62).

In *All Together Now* and *Notes for Another Life* Bridgers skips a generation, a pattern she essentially follows in the still-to-come *Sara Will* and *Permanent Connections*. *Notes for Another Life* includes a paragraph that offers almost a summary of the feelings of the older women Bridgers has placed in charge of the youngsters in their care. Bliss is preparing dinner and awaiting the arrival of Bill, Kevin, and Wren. "They would sit together at the table in front of the dark window, the glowing light above their heads like a beacon to remind them that this was where they each belonged. Here, together, but with a generation missing. There would be no extra places, though. No obvious reminders that once there had been six places for Sunday dinner. And yet, they would all remember because there was no washing away memory. Karen would be there. And Tom. And the inherent sadness of empty places" (43).

The strong older women she had already created foreshadowed Bridgers's next novel, in which her focus is primarily on an older woman, her titular character. Sara Will is not always easy for readers to like. Headstrong, set in her ways, with convictions that border on selfishness, not particularly kind to others or much interested in their problems, Sara Will presents a considerable challenge to a writer: how to make her the kind of woman Fate Jessop would want to marry and readers would want to read about. Bridgers may have been more successful with managing Fate's judgments than her readers'. Fate does marry Sara Will. The reading public has been somewhat more indifferent. Sales of the book have been limited and it has not received that sine qua non of fictional success, a paperback version.

All the more irony, then, that this highly skilled writer would see so much of herself in Sara Will, yet fail, at least from a commercial perspective, to be able to present that character to a wide audience of readers. Of Sara Will, the woman, not the novel, Bridgers says, "Sara was sort of a manifestation of all my hidden stuff, because of all the things she was afraid of. All of those fears are fears that I have. It's just that I've got enough social skills and was brought up to overcome the fears. She couldn't overcome them, so they were just sticking right out all over her."[16] Sara Will possesses some of this same kind of introspection: "I have been alone too long, she thought. Too long to change. Yet her unyielding nature wasn't something she was pleased with or proud of. She hadn't intended to be unbending; one doesn't plan from birth to be set in one's ways. A person just takes hold of those attributes that seem most reasonable" (113).

Bridgers has created in Sara Will an extraordinarily complex woman. One must exercise caution not to judge a book on the likability of its central characters, on whether they are the kinds of folks one would choose as friends. Fate and Swanee Hope aside, people may not much like Sara Will, but careful readers must admire the patience, the attention, the love, the thought that went into her creation. Unhappily the marginal sales success of this novel has prevented many students of fiction from getting acquainted with a singular literary creation.

Permanent Connections alters the pattern slightly. The wise older woman is not all that old, nor is she directly connected to main character Rob Dickson. Yet she is memorable enough to be counted along with Jane and Bliss, Maggie and Sara Will. She is Ginny Collier, Ellery's mother, a woman who has divorced her husband, left Charlotte, and moved to rural Tyler Mills for a better life, one she fervently hopes her daughter will come to share. She and Ellery exist somewhat tumultuously, their trial and tribulation caused in large part by Ellery's reluctance to accept living in the hinterlands after spending her first fifteen years in the exciting big city. But Ginny values patience. In a carefully drawn extended metaphor that reviewer Barbara Chatton called "heartbreakingly lovely"[17] Bridgers depicts Ginny thinking of her work at her weaving loom as kindred to her work as a parent: "It had been one of her hardest adjustments to weaving—not being able to view the product until it was finished. Once the piece was done, the warp cut, and the cloth unwound from the beam, there was no changing it, no going back. You had to live with what you'd made. It is the same with children, Ginny thought" (72–73).

Ginny's relationship with the protagonist Rob is less fully treated, but she has an obvious impact. It is she whom he calls after wrecking Fairlee's truck and being arrested for possession of marijuana. Later, he quietly marvels at her ability to be both warm and candid. She could, he notices, touch his aged grandfather with ease and affection, be honest and frank with Fairlee, tender with Coralee. Fearless, Rob calls her. He learns, too, from her model to be as much at peace with himself as possible, to act on how he feels.

Ginny also takes on the noble but extremely difficult task of helping Rob's Aunt Coralee overcome her agoraphobia. She begins with their shared interest in sewing. Even there Coralee's agoraphobic tendencies reveal themselves. Commenting on the borders she puts on everything she sews—towels, curtains, throw rugs—Coralee says, "I close everything up. You put a good binding around it and it's sealed. Can't nothing get through it" (94). Ginny tries on a jacket that Coralee has made for her and moves to see the jacket in the light, Coralee following her. First they go to the back door, then to the porch. Not for long, to be sure, as she later tells Ellery, "two minutes at the most, but it's a start" (165).

If novels had background music, Coralee's emergence would best be accompanied by Beethoven's "Ode to Joy." Her victory over agoraphobia comes slowly, but it comes, largely because Ginny helps out and discusses some of her own concerns with Coralee. They are talking, significantly on the porch, one day and Coralee laments that Rob has been the cause of trouble almost from the day he came to Tyler Mills. In her response Ginny not only shares Coralee's worries about Rob but reveals her own about Ellery. She says that Ellery is too serious, Rob too flighty and moody, but they need time and nurture and they will make it. They are learning. Just like us, she then adds, referring to herself and Coralee. We are learning and we will make it.

And so the wisdom and patience first seen in Maggie Grover and later in Jane and Bliss is found again in Ginny: they handle adolescents well, even when the adolescents are agoraphobes in their fifties. These women whom Bridgers has created are, she has said, both her challenge and her opportunity. She speaks of a sign she frequently saw: "On my way across North Carolina, I used to pass a billboard that seemed to be there just for me. 'There is not a heavier burden than a great opportunity.' I squirmed a little because I knew even then what my great opportunity was —to illuminate the lives of rural people, especially the women of my family."[18]

The Minor Characters

In T. S. Eliot's "Lovesong of J. Alfred Prufrock" the dispirited Prufrock places himself in the total scheme of things:

> No! I am not Prince Hamlet, nor was meant to be;
> Am an attendant lord, one that will do
> To swell a progress, start a scene or two,
> Advise the prince. . . .

Prufrock is, in other words, one of life's minor characters.

Fiction has its minor characters, too. Often in young adult literature they serve stereotypic roles, swelling scenes, adding background murmurs, seldom doing much to enhance the novels they are placed in. Not so, however, in the novels of Sue Ellen Bridgers. Though it would be overstatement (and overlong) to treat all of her minor characters as if each was worthy of extensive attention, certain of them do merit a glance of some significance.

As mentioned earlier, reviewer Katherine Paterson likened *All Together Now* to a novelistic square dance with four couples exchanging turns—Jane and Ben, Casey and Dwayne, Pansy and Hazard, Taylor and Gwen.[19] Each of these couples is well drawn, fleshed out. Even though some of them—Ben, Taylor, Gwen— receive smaller amounts of printer's ink, readers know them, can identify with them. Taylor lives for his Mercury and his racing, Gwen for Taylor, Ben for his evenings of calm on the front porch. More important roles are played by Hazard and Pansy. Hazard, in fact, was the first character described by Bridgers when she began *All Together Now*; she saw him "dancing on the porch, a

visual image of a friend's grandfather."[20] His relationship with
Pansy, the pathos of their honeymoon, and his attempt to win
her back almost take over this novel. The most compelling minor
character in *All Together Now* is Dwayne. Retarded, with a twelve-
year-old mind in a thirty-three-year-old body, he has an ebulli-
ence, a simple joy in all that he does. Readers get to know Dwayne,
but never find him out of character, intelligent beyond the limited
mental equipment Bridgers has given him. It cannot be an easy
task to portray a retarded adult without slipping into sentimentality or inconsistency. Bridgers avoids both pitfalls.

Unlike those many novelists who write for adolescents and who
use a limited first-person perspective, Bridgers writes in the third-
person omniscient point of view and moves from character to
character, telling more about some than about others—there are
only so many pages—but telling enough about almost all of them
that they take on fully human dimensions. It is her objective:
"Bringing the internal lives of several characters to your attention
in one story is perhaps an unrealistic goal but the temptation to
do just that is so overpowering that I generally succumb to it."[21]
She has been criticized for her shifting point of view, particularly
with *All Together Now*.[22] The cavil invites debate. There is clearly
compelling drama in the relationship between Hazard and Pansy
and in whether Dwayne will remain in the town or be taken to
the hospital. It helps readers to be privy to these concerns, to
share Hazard's doubts about his social clumsiness, Pansy's em-
barrassed worries about their marriage, the whole community's
outrage at what might happen to Dwayne. To write of but one
character, Bridgers says, could become boring; she prefers to explore several characters in one novel, to have multiple perspec-
tives.[23]

This pattern of creating absorbing minor characters began with
Home before Dark, which is Stella's story mainly, but not hers
alone. The novel offers its readers a less intense but no less real
look at many diverse characters—Mae, unable to face a new life;
Maggie, eager for one; James Earl and Newton, uneasy in their
long-discarded sibling relationship; Anne, watchful over them all,
especially Stella. They all have their stories to tell, too, and

Bridgers so depicts them that they take on the uniqueness of real people. Readers can see Mae's skinny and worn hands, her unshaven legs, her faded dresses and her shoes with the broken laces, and share the incongruity she must feel in the presence of the immaculately groomed Anne. Like anyone given to second thoughts, Maggie worries about the instant motherhood that will be conferred upon her when she and James Earl marry. James Earl and Newton cement anew their brotherly affections when they stare together at the blood-stained mattress where their mother committed suicide to end her cancer-stricken life. Anne uses Stella as a kind of dry run for her own approaching baby. In Bridgers's careful hands, even in this first novel, her minor characters are fully fleshed out.

Notes for Another Life also has important minor characters, but less completely realized ones, making it for that reason as well as others a less effective novel. Wren's boyfriend Sam never quite emerges from a goody-two-shoes stereotype and both Tom and Karen need more development. One wants to know more about Tom's mental imbalances and Karen's quest for a life in the fast lanes of Atlanta. How much did Tom's periodic bouts of insane depression fuel Karen's desire for a life away from him, and vice versa? The Reverend Jack Kensley seems too much the turtle-necked minister spending a shortish tenure in the hinterlands and, while there, providing pop psychology to Kevin; it must be said, however, that his advice is sound and does help Kevin.

Two of the better-drawn characters in *Notes for Another Life* are Kevin's early girlfriend Melanie and Wren's friend Jolene, the latter one of Bridgers's favorites among her minor figures. Both seem typically teenage. Melanie's ever-watering eyes ruin all of her attempts with mascara, but do not blur them so much that she cannot sense Jolene's youthful interest in Kevin. To him Jolene is just his kid sister's little friend, the one who tries on every possible outfit in every possible store and never buys anything. To her Kevin is a perfect ten. In the end of the novel Bridgers provides just a hint that these two very appealing teens might come together. And she lets Melanie down carefully, as, after

Kevin's suicide attempt, Melanie thinks that just being friends will be sufficient for her and Kevin.

Five characters make up the cast of *Sara Will*. Three of them —Sara herself, Eva, and Michael—were discussed earlier. Mention must still be made of Fate, short for Lafayette, Jessop, and of Sara Will's sister, Swanee Hope. Both are vivid, memorable. The dissolution of Fate's not particularly happy life when Eva descends on him results in a newly born man. One-armed, not overly quick-witted, but blessed with a good heart, Fate sets out, first, to protect Eva, then later to woo Sara Will. He succeeds in both endeavors and does so in ways that win readers' hearts. He first helps Eva with her pregnancy, getting the local midwife to do the actual delivery but being around through it all, as nervous as if he were the expectant father. Then he gets them both to Sara Will's, where he is determined they will be no bother. That is, until he falls in love with Sara and wants to be a bother. He joins her for morning breakfast that he prepares, then respects her desire for silence. Ignoring his handicap, he chops the wood for the winter, polishes Sara Will's beloved 1968 Mustang, and even initially agrees with her that he and Eva and, later, Michael cannot stay. But he knows that they, or at least he, will.

The widowed Swanee Hope, reduced to life back at the old homestead where her younger sister has ruled supreme for all these years, manages both to get her own way a good bit of the time and gain the attention and affection of readers while she is doing it. She watches television game shows, knowing that they bore Sara. She demands that they host a Christmas party, knowing that Sara will likely become apoplectic at the thought. She insists that Fate and Eva be allowed to stay, first for a meal, then overnight, then a few weeks, and then as long as they need to, knowing that their presence will annoy Sara. Yet there is never any doubt that she loves Sara Will, just as Sara Will loves her. When Fate and Sara marry, Swanee Hope has the good sense to clear out for an extended visit to her son's family in California, where she even becomes a contestant on one of her favorite television game shows.

A number of minor characters in *Permanent Connections* round out the plot and illuminate the other characters. Rob's cousin Leanna, having gone steady with Travis practically since both of them were born, provides a needed sounding board for Ellery to discuss her developing love for Rob. Leanna is matter-of-fact about her sexual activity with Travis, reflecting a more modern teenage viewpoint about sex than found in Bridgers's earlier novels. Aunt Rosalie acts as a one-voice chorus of disapproval, both of Rob and of his father, ironically strengthening their tenuous relationship. Aunt Coralee's agoraphobia is a disease that Bridgers *shows*, not merely names. Readers can sense Coralee's fears about leaving the house and, when she goes to the hospital with her injured father, her emotional priorities are given a different and believable order. Most memorable is Uncle Fairlee, whose disabling broken hip sets the novel in motion. He is wise and shares that wisdom with Rob. For example, though he does not fully understand the reasons for his sister's mental illness, he sensitively tries to explain it to Rob: "That's the worst kind of thing to be afraid of. Something in your head" (87).

Bridgers's minor characters go well beyond Prufrock's limiting vision of his own role. Like him, they swell a progress, begin a scene; unlike him, they add to it in important and useful ways. She tells a little about each of them, provides an idiosyncratic habit or a personality quirk, so that they are far from the stereotypic minor characters of much fiction, simply background figures of little significance.

Bridgers's characters—her adolescents, her older women, her minor figures—interest her readers for a variety of reasons. They have problems that are believable. They are themselves believable. Generally middle-class folks whose lives lack the excitement of big city living or cosmological issues that need resolution—no Bridgers character will stop a war by retrieving the stolen battle plans in time or discover the cure for cancer—they are more like us than not. They are common people, like most of Bridgers's readers. The identifications are quick and easy. Adolescents particularly are drawn to Bridgers's novels because they know adolescents like those she portrays. They go to school with a Jolene who has a crush on her best friend's older brother. They see in Rob a fellow teenager whose relationships with his parents have almost totally disintegrated. Like Kevin and Ellery, they know, either firsthand or through experiences of their friends, the unending pain of parental separation.

But the principal reason for the compelling attention Bridgers is able to get for her characters derives from one simple fact: they interest her. As she says of them:

> I can't write about people who don't interest me. Imagine the boredom, not to mention irritation, of spending a year with people you don't like. One of the reasons I like my characters is that I'm interested in the problems they have. Problem solving is the key to characterization. Somebody wants or needs something important and the writer investigates their journey toward that goal. The struggle is as valuable as the result. In real life we frequently don't get what we want but hopefully we learn something, we meet a challenge in such a way that we grow and change. That's all I ask of my characters. They don't have to find happy endings, just new beginnings.[24]

4. A Study of Themes

"I do not consider a work of fiction the appropriate place for my personal causes or point of view," Sue Ellen Bridgers has said. "I am writing a story, revealing someone else's experience. I am not writing a homily, an article, or a speech. When I'm writing fiction, what I think has to be secondary. What the character feels and does is primary."[1]

Maybe so; maybe not. Christopher Isherwood points out, "Every writer has certain subjects that they write about again and again, and most people's books are just variations on certain themes." So it appears with Bridgers's novels and stories. Though presented with twists, written "with a slant," as Emily Dickinson said, these themes are found commonly enough to suggest that Bridgers does have causes and points of view that permeate her fiction, whether she wants them to or not. These merit further attention.

Love

Throughout Bridgers's work one finds extraordinary examples of love. It is not always the romantic, sexually driven love that dominates Norma Klein's novels for young adults, nor the strong friendships between peers that Paul Zindel portrays so frequently and convincingly. Rather, the love motif in Bridgers's work appears in many shapes and forms: the sexual attraction Rob has for Ellery in *Permanent Connections*, the feelings of comfort and security between Bliss and Bill in *Notes for Another Life*, the troubled uncertainty that accompanies this entirely new feeling of love Sara Will is experiencing, the whole town's love for Dwayne in *All Together Now*.

Although she denies the intrusion of her own values, Bridgers does recognize the importance of love in her novels. She speaks of a guiding principle placed on a note card in her den:

> On the wall beside my desk, there is a quote from Teilhard de Chardin which reads: "Someday after we have mastered the winds, the waves, the tides and gravity, we shall harness for God the energies of love. Then, for the second time in the history of the world, man will have discovered fire."
> It is there to remind me that love is energy.[2]

And so love is found in Bridgers's books, not so much as an act in itself but as a catalyst. Love is the sustaining solace that Jane has in *All Together Now* that permits her to be a source of comfort to everyone around her. It is the urgent need Ginny has in *Permanent Connections* that impels her to go beyond herself to help Coralee. Love really means, in a Bridgers work, being important to someone. As Casey reflects on Pansy's wedding day in *All Together Now*, "Pansy would remember that she had been special to somebody, and there wasn't any better feeling than that" (82).

The someones to whom someone else is special are many and varied in Bridgers's novels. There is the love between parent and child. "I love you, Daddy" Stella says to James Earl in *Home before Dark* after he has broken the difficult news of his impending marriage to Maggie and, by that one assertion, she reassures him that what he is doing is all right (143). Wren in *Notes for Another Life* attends church with her mentally ill father Tom and realizes that, despite her having grown up without a real father because of his illness, she loves him still, "this man whose fingers now clung to hers, and by doing so, she had risked rejection, denial, indifference. Yet here he was sitting beside her" (153). Throughout his adolescent years Rob's relationship with his father in *Permanent Connections* has been a troubled one, mostly because of his own intransigence. Yet when Rob has caused his grandfather's accident and is soon to be on trial for drug possession, his father Davis is there and a bond between them is cemented, a bond of love.

Love also appears between husband and wife, or between those about to become married. Yet it is not the hot-blooded, fiery passion of two teenagers unable or unwilling to control their primal urges. Rather, it is more typically a love between older people. That love is, of course, sexual, but not only or primarily that. Maggie and James Earl discuss sex in *Home before Dark*, early in their courtship: " 'I know nothing about love,' she said after awhile. 'No, that's not true. I think I know a great deal about love, but nothing about sex. Maybe I'm too old.' 'And maybe,' James Earl said, 'when we're young we know too much about sex and too little about love' " (131).

If love means being special to somebody, then few exemplify this definition more than Jane and Ben in *All Together Now*:

> Jane knew she was still in love with Ben. *In love*. That was what she meant, although she'd have a hard time saying it, even to him. It was so much easier just to say she loved him. After all, she had spent years loving him, taking care of him. Her dedication to him and their sons had consumed her, energized her, probably even aged her, but still she was in love with him, could feel giddy when she looked out from the church choir to see him looking back at her. (68)

Like the relationship between Jane and Ben, the one between Bliss and Bill in *Notes for Another Life* reveals itself in their every interaction, a love born more of respect and affection than of unbridled passion. They had been through much together, the up-and-down illness of a cherished only son, the departure (desertion? Bliss sometimes wondered) of a daughter-in-law they had welcomed as if she were their own child, the taking in of their two grandchildren when their best parenting years were well behind them. Yet through it all one feature of their lives had remained constant—the love between them. That had sustained them.

Two more couples among the older folks Bridgers writes about show still another dimension of love: Pansy and Hazard, who marry after their twenty-five-year courtship in *All Together Now*, and Sara Will and Fate in *Sara Will*, whose marriage may be even more unlikely. Left too much to Hazard's clumsy hands, the beginning of his and Pansy's marriage proves almost to be its end. Yet they endure, brought together by Hazard's refusal to be spurned and by Pansy's ultimate recognition that he merits her love. Sara Will and Fate have not been courting, indeed have not even seen or thought of each other for many years until Fate descends on Sara Will's house. Once he is there, however, their attraction for each other quickens. Despite Sara's almost physically willing it not to happen, it does. And when Fate finally says he loves her, "the sound of it broke over her like a silky wave she would drown in" (235). Bridgers can allow them to marry (she worried about whether they should get married), for theirs will be a good life together.

Teenagers in Bridgers's books also feel special to each other. Toby and Stella fall in a sort of love in *Home before Dark*, though aware that they have many years and, probably, many other loves ahead of them. Ringing a little less true is the relationship between Wren and Sam in *Notes for Another Life*. They experience what amounts to mid-life crises while Wren is still in grade school as she wonders how Sam will accommodate his desire for a wife who may on occasion give piano lessons while she yearns for the concert stage. The most fully developed teenage relationship in Bridgers's works and the one best described is that of Rob and Ellery in *Permanent Connections*. It includes the one sexual encounter between her adolescent characters. (That intimacy is discreetly described; Bridgers confesses to uneasiness when writing about sex.[3]) Rob and Ellery disagree about its meaning. To him their act signals more than it does to her. He owns her, he thinks, can have her whenever he wants. To her it is too much too soon, and she demands that they back off, give each other more time.

Bridgers hedges a bit about them at the end of the novel, providing readers a choice about whether they stay together or not. Her own mind is certain, however: "Their future is somewhat open-ended but hopeful. Together or separate, they have grown. They have influenced each other's lives. They are better for having known each other. This may not be realistic, but being the romantic that I am, I share the conviction of many young people that they are together still. We all need the possibility of a happy ending."[4]

Finally, there is love between friends, that awareness that you are special to someone not bound to you by kinship or sexual attraction. In Bridgers's novels that special kind of love is revealed most memorably in the companionship between Casey and Dwayne in *All Together Now*. Though begun on a note of duplicity, the relationship between them soon becomes an example of fast friendship, the enduring and forgiving kind. "The only way to have a friend," wrote Emerson, "is to be one." Casey and Dwayne are friends in exactly this sense. Dwayne, for all his mental limitations, has given some thought to his relations with others. He tells Casey, "You be nice to folks and they be nice to you right back. That's one thing for sure" (52). Later, when Dwayne is rescued by the friendship of virtually the entire town, Casey recognizes that he is indeed "wrapped in love" (210). Emerson also wrote, "A friend is a person with whom I may be sincere." Few friendships in fiction better exemplify this principle than Jane and Pansy's.

Friendship appears in Bridgers's other writing as well. Wren and Jolene are best friends in *Notes for Another Life*, even after Wren finds Sam. The open Leanna and the doubtful Ellery so trust each other in *Permanent Connections* that they can discuss that most private and worrisome of teenage subjects, sex. In that same novel Ginny and Uncle Fairlee have become fast friends in the short time Ginny and Ellery have lived in the mountains.

Love, then, remains a central theme in Bridgers's writing, as a number of reviewers have noted.[5] She handles it well, as might be expected given her capacity for loving friends and family, about whom she often speaks. Two examples: In a speech she has given several times to audiences of teachers and students, she says, "I remember once when our three children were home for a holiday and we were all crowded in one small kitchen talking to each other, all completely in the moment, when suddenly tears sprang to my eyes and I felt this incredible flood of well-being and gratitude that we were together and no matter what ills afflicted the world, at that moment we were whole."[6] Of friendship she has said, "Friendship, a reciprocal, compromising business, requires diligence, and sometimes the effort seems to outweigh the rewards and the attempt at friendship fails. At other times friendship blossoms and a commitment of time and care results."[7] The importance of family and of friends in her personal life is simply but touchingly demonstrated on the dedication page of *Sara Will*:

For Ben

In Memoriam

Annie McGlohon Abbott
1887–1983

Nancye Smathers Haire
1938–1981

Ben is, of course, her husband. Abbott was her maternal grandmother. Haire was a best friend and college classmate who committed suicide.

One of her major characters, Jane Flanagan in *All Together Now*, summarizes Bridgers's view well: "Loving is truly the biggest risk a person can take, and the one that's most worth it" (73). And one of her reviewers provides an echo: "Without being Pollyanna Bridgers departs from the current norm of despair by championing brotherhood and love."[8]

Families

Tolstoy began *Anna Karenina* with an assertion that has since become famous: "Happy families are all alike; every unhappy family is unhappy in its own way." Judith Guest, author of the acclaimed novel *Ordinary People*, writes, "I have often been asked why it is that I only write about dysfunctional families. The answer that comes to mind is, what other kinds are there?"[9] Despite the love that permeates her novels Bridgers clearly portrays unhappy, dysfunctional families in much of her writing. As in Tolstoy's fiction, the unhappiness has particular causes and effects.

It needs to be pointed out that this reference is to the nuclear family—mom, dad, the kids—and not to the extended family that includes grandparents, uncles, aunts, and assorted cousins. An interesting rhetorical device exists here: to repair the nuclear family, Bridgers creates an extended family that almost borders on the supernormal, the too good. Though she denies basing her writing on her own youthful life, that kind of intra- and intergenerational mix marked her younger years. Her father's repeated bouts with mental illness forced her mother to do double duty and created all kinds of unhappiness, but much of it was leavened by the geographic and emotional proximity of her grandmothers. Thus, to find grandmothers (or their surrogates) playing major roles in an extended family in a Bridgers novel is not surprising.

No nuclear family in Bridgers's writing is unhappier than the Jacksons in *Notes for Another Life*. Tom, in and out of the mental institution, recognizes his weaknesses, his inability to be the father he would like his children to have, the husband Karen ought to be married to. Such awareness exacerbates his mental instability. Karen agonizes over her desertion of her children for Atlanta's business world. Kevin experiences more difficulty than his younger sister Wren in playing the hand that fate dealt him. Why, he repeatedly asks, should *he* have a father who is mentally ill, a mother who appears not to love her children? He gets no answers that he can understand until after the failed suicide attempt when he realizes that whatever Tom and Karen are, it is not his fault. In her role in the extended family Grandmother Bliss provides the emotional glue that holds everything together, even if precariously.

Bridgers's earlier *All Together Now* hinted at this theme of troubled nuclear families, but somewhat vaguely. Casey's father

David has a legitimate reason for his absence; he is flying planes in wartime Korea. But the generational skip effected by the absence of Casey's mother needs better explanation than Bridgers offers. Mom is back home where she has taken a second job. Why? Does the family need the money? (Curiously, money is seldom a problem for any of Bridgers's characters, even the migrant Willis family in *Home before Dark*.) And that second job is a bit suspect—singing in a night club. For this kind of work she would send her only daughter away for the summer? Readers do not know. For most of the novel she is a puzzling blank. Even when her daughter has what might be polio, she does not get involved. At first she is not told of her daughter's illness. When she does learn that Casey is out of danger, she still elects not to visit this child who experienced a potentially fatal ordeal. Again, the extended family, most notably grandmother Jane, supplies the love and wisdom Casey needs.

In *Permanent Connections* the pattern repeats itself with only minor variations. Rob's mother, a college professor, worries about his drifting and nearly delinquent behavior in the opening pages of the novel, then is heard no more, not even coming to the trial that could result in Rob's imprisonment. Father Davis saddles Rob with the task of caring for his grandfather, Uncle Fairlee, and Aunt Coralee, and it is these members of the extended family, particularly Fairlee, who furnish Rob the adult models he needs. Again, a troubled nuclear family, a healthy extended one.

To a lesser extent the theme exists in *Home before Dark*, where Mae's impact on her children, and on all life around her, is minimal, and in *Sara Will*, where Eva's family, notwithstanding the possibly jaundiced description of them provided by Eva, nonetheless seem destructive. Again members of an extended family rescue the adolescents—Aunt Anne and Maggie for Stella in the first novel, Fate for Eva in the second.

Juxtaposing the themes of love and troubled families has to present some technical difficulties for a writer who has deep feelings about love and about her family, present and past. On the one hand is the desire to promote love as a theme worthy of fictional study. Yet an author needs a plot, something happening.

Bridgers has developed a method that she can use in compelling ways in her writing. Love may be present in her nuclear families, but it is difficult to express: Mae is shy; Casey's parents are absent; Tom is mentally ill, Karen otherwise engaged; Rob's parents are temporarily out of his life (and his hair). Others, then, people from the extended family can come forward to offer the love that all adolescents need, whether they always recognize that need or not. Bridgers makes the plan work.

Mental Illness

Sue Ellen Bridgers grew up with mental illness and mental illness plays a part in every one of her novels. The forms may differ, but the psychoses are there.

In *Home before Dark* Mae is the sufferer. Shy, unsophisticated, dependent all her life on James Earl, Mae exhibits a form of agoraphobia that later afflicted to a degree the title character in *Sara Will* and came to full revelation in the behavior of Coralee in *Permanent Connections*. Yet Mae's agoraphobia—a fear of open or public places—is the opposite of Sara Will's and Coralee's. While they are unable to leave a place, their houses, Mae is unable to stay. Conditioned by a life on the road that has had her moving to a new migrant camp every few weeks, she finds the permanence of the Willis farm too much to bear. Aware of her mental state, she whispers, "I've got to get out of here" (50).

Mae does "get out": she dies. It seems so much a relief for her that Stella wonders if people like Mae really want to die and, a few days later, tells Toby her conclusion: "I think Mama stood there waiting to get struck down. I think she let it happen because she didn't like it here" (103).

Sara Will is neither a reprint of Mae, nor a precursor of Coralee, and it may be stretching a point to label her behavior agoraphobic. Bridgers herself allows that the label is apt in Sara Will's case, saying that she "is agoraphobic in that she will not get off her own property."[10] In a fitting description of Sara Will the novel reads "When she felt comfortable, she saw no point in disturbing things, and she had always been comfortable in her worn clothes and her aging house" (5). Later, when Sara Will, Swanee Hope, Eva, and baby Rachel go out for a rare evening, it is Sara who most fears "going into the restaurant, ordering food, eating while other people talked and ate around her. She wasn't sure she'd know how to behave. What if she were forced by panic to rise and flee to the restroom or the parking lot?" (146). Embodying her name, Sara Will willfully remains in control, and if the evening is not entirely a success, neither is it an embarrassing failure. Her love for Fate finally overcomes her agoraphobia, but echoes linger even then. When Fate wrecks her beloved old-but-still-new Mustang, she leaves him temporarily, going to Tyler Mills and taking a room in a boardinghouse, yet she rarely departs from it until she returns home several days later.

Full-blown agoraphobia strikes Coralee shortly after her mother's death, prior to the beginning of *Permanent Connections*. Early in the novel Ellery explains and names the condition for Rob (and, in so doing, conveniently explains it to any puzzled readers):

> "I think she's got agoraphobia."
> "She's got what?"
> "Agoraphobia. She hasn't been out of the house in at least three years. Not even in the yard." (41)

Uncle Fairlee explains to Rob that the onset of the disease had been sudden. Coralee had been in the backyard, hanging the wash, when Fairlee overheard what he calls a "wailing sound" coming from her. Next he noticed her stand motionless for a minute, then rush into the house, and "far as I know, she ain't been out of the house since" (87).

Ginny's patient and kind treatment triumphs and Coralee finally emerges, first to the porch, then to her yard, and, ultimately to the great world beyond. Curing Coralee is, for Ginny, however, more than a Samaritan gesture; she also helps cure herself. Earlier, after a fight with Ellery and while thinking of Coralee's behavior, she whispered to the darkness: "I am afraid, too. Hear me, Coralee Dickson, while you are curled like an animal in a hole away from the sky and wind and sun. The demons that devour women are all the same" (92).

Bridgers visits upon two male characters mental disorders of even greater proportions than those of her agoraphobic women, aberrations that require their periodic removal from society. Most severely damaged is Tom in *Notes for Another Life*. In and out of institutions for almost a decade, more in than out, a victim of failed shock treatments, Tom does get home once during the novel and, hope again betraying reason, all his loved ones think that maybe, just maybe, this will be the time he will be cured. Tom himself is encouraged. He tells Wren, "I think I've got a grip on a lot of things this time, honey" (140). But Tom, too, deludes himself. After the false starts he falls back into old ways and has to be institutionalized again. Realistically Bridgers holds out little hope for any kind of permanent cure.

In *All Together Now* Dwayne is the retarded adult male every stereotyped small town has. "Wouldn't hurt a fly," folks say of him. "You can trust him with all you got." In Dwayne's case the cliché becomes the fact. Dwayne wins the hearts of readers as quickly as he has already won those of his neighborhood and town. Clumsy of foot, halting of speech, yet ebulliently happy and always ready to help, Dwayne will forever be a twelve-year-old to whom Bridgers ascribes a twelve-year-old's interests: baseball most of all, Saturday afternoon matinees at the local Bijou, a yearning to be able to drive a car. However, charming though he may be, perhaps even a curiosity, Dwayne needs care. There is only so much his mother can do, only so much friends can help out with. Ultimately Dwayne may have to return to the mental asylum he so detests. Alva may have the final word, after all. But in the climactic moment of *All Together Now* the community, led by Taylor and Jane, say "not yet." Dwayne will remain a part of the little town that is his, too, for a while longer.

It is important to note the connection between the themes of love and mental illness in Bridgers's novels. In every one in which there is a mentally ill character there are other characters who care deeply for him or her. That same sympathetic caring was a reality in her own childhood, during her father's mental illness.[11]

Connections

In literature written by Sue Ellen Bridgers those who love connect, the present members of families, the mentally ill, the good friends. But there are further connections with previous generations, bygone ones. In many novels written for teenagers the present is paramount, all there is. Readers do not know if characters even have grandparents or if they feel in any way connected to those who have gone before them. They know in a Bridgers piece of fiction.

Early in *Home before Dark* Newton tells James Earl of their mother's suicide; this information establishes their connection with the past. Middle-aged Pansy often thinks of her father in *All Together Now*, even comparing some of his less favorable behaviors with Hazard's. In *Notes for Another Life* Bliss frequently recalls how close she was to her mother: "She remembered sleepless nights when she was a little girl and would come down to find her mother still about.... They had talked then, while the house clucked and sighed around them. Her mother had given her absolute attention, and so in the night unexpected words had passed between them, mother and child, as they spoke of minute concerns, daily worries that hampered them, the wistful dreams of girls, the unquenchable hopes of mothers" (59).

Sara Will lives, too, with her connections, caring for the cemetery where her parents lie buried, thinking often of her annoying inability to cross the lake to the island cemetery where her sister Serena is buried. The climactic moment of *Sara Will* is, in fact, when Fate takes Sara Will to the island so that she can tend to Serena's long-ignored grave site.

Bridgers actually uses the word "connections," most notably, of course, in the title of her fifth novel. Those connections for Rob do not become permanent until the end of the novel, but there the implication is clear that, whether he remains in Tyler Mills or returns to New Jersey, he has become a part of the Dickson family. It is not the first time Bridgers has thought about literal connections in her novels. In *Notes for Another Life* the Jackson family, including father Tom, attends church and, when Tom gives

Kevin five dollars for the collection plate, Kevin, for the first time in years, feels "explicitly his connection to his parent" (156). Ironically, Karen senses the same feeling in that novel, calling Kevin and Wren "the only connection" she has any more (211), even as she admits that she cannot change her life.

From an author so wedded to her own past, to the significance in her life of her grandmothers, to the strong relationship with her mother, to her nurturance of and gratification from husband and children and friends, such connections seem natural. But she deliberately searches them out in her writing, as evidenced by this discussion of how she came to know Rob Dickson for the novel *Permanent Connections*:

> Drawing him out was partially a matter of uncovering his past. How did you get this way? I kept asking him. What is your family history? So I discovered his grandfather on a homeplace in the southern Appalachians of North Carolina, a man . . . who resents change and God and his son who has grown away from the family. And that son, Rob's father, who has a corporate job the home folks don't understand or appreciate, a college-professor wife, and two children who know next to nothing about their heritage. Even if Rob had never gone to North Carolina, I still would have needed to know this grandfather and this father—they are part of who Rob is; they are among his most powerful connections.[12]

The Outsider

Only in *Notes for Another Life* does Bridgers create an intact community, one without interlopers from the outside, and even in that one she has Karen making periodic visits from Atlanta. In Bridgers's other novels, however, the outsider frequently assumes center stage and acts catalytically on the rest of the cast.

Stella in *Home before Dark* comes from a background of nights spent in station wagons, days spent in orange groves, to the community of her father and his forebears. Once there, she feels her roots, her connections, and vows not to leave. She also changes life for those she meets, Toby, Rodney Biggers, her Aunt Anne, Maggie Grover. Casey provides the same thematic plot device in *All Together Now*. Initially, she is Dwayne's baseball partner and Jane and Ben's summer joy. Later, Casey voices the outrage of the entire community at Dwayne's potential return to the mental institution and galvanizes neighborhood concern and sympathy when her fever is thought to be polio. Sara Will is the protagonist of the novel *Sara Will*, but she shares that billing with Fate, an outsider who wreaks considerable havoc in her patterned life before she succumbs to the charms of this one-armed man and agrees to marry him. Rob and Ellery must be dragged kicking and screaming into the protective warmth and custody of Tyler Mills in *Permanent Connections*, but first they make their mark. Rob wrecks Uncle Fairlee's car, gets arrested on a drug possession charge, causes his grandfather's near death. Ellery's consistent unhappiness and yearning for Charlotte make Ginny question whether her divorce and move to the country were sensible.

Not infrequently the outsider motif permits Bridgers to contrast small-town life with that of the bigger city her outsiders left. Casey lives in a coastal city, Fate in a town much larger than Tyler Mills, Rob in urban New Jersey, Ellery in bustling Charlotte, but all of them succumb to the charms Bridgers places in her small towns—and believes herself are there.

The Role of Women

She marched in rural Sylva for the Equal Rights Amendment. She says she "didn't know a Republican until she was grown"; Winterville was Democrat country, Kennedy land.[13] Yet Bridgers is cautious about labeling herself a feminist. Such self-identification may not be necessary. Her books tell the story, by commissions and omissions.

First, the omissions. In most of her writing the males are less effective, less instrumental in what goes on than the females. It is Maggie who resolutely goes after the newly bereft James Earl in *Home before Dark*, chasing him just fast enough so that he can catch her. Ben and Bill are only background characters in *All Together Now* and *Notes for Another Life*. In the former novel Casey's Uncle Taylor plays a larger role, but even in his grand scene, the town council meeting, it is Jane whose understanding Alva seeks and she whose passion to let Dwayne stay carries the day. Neither Fate in *Sara Will* nor Hazard in *All Together Now* has ever amounted to much and their futures do not look much brighter until they decide to marry.

Bridgers's response to questions about these omissions of strong men in her novels reflects her own childhood. The men are away from home—at work.[14] James Earl toils in the tobacco fields with brother Newton, as did the men in Bridgers's family. Ben owns a lumberyard, Bill a drugstore. Fate defines himself through work, at least until he leaves his job to travel to Tyler Mills. Economically the men must be viewed as successful; still, the impression lingers that it is the women who call the tune, at least the family melody.

Wise beyond her years, Stella comforts her father more than the other way around when Mae dies in *Home before Dark*; soon Maggie Grover steps in. Jane is a central character in *All Together Now*, facilitating both the marriage, then the reconciliation of Pansy and Hazard, providing a moral presence for the entire community in the Alva/Dwayne confrontation, watching over the stricken Casey until the fever breaks. Her characterization provides a writer's rehearsal for Bliss, who plays much the same role in *Notes for Another Life*. Like Jane, Bliss is happy in her marriage, worried about her son's marriage, and determined that her grandchildren will be well reared. Then, in the chronology of Bridgers's novels, come Sara Will and Ginny in *Permanent Connections*, both strong women, though given to self-doubt, Sara about her own rigidity, Ginny about her emotional demons.

Only on occasion does Bridgers directly confront the contemporary role of women, most obviously in *Notes for Another Life* and *Permanent Connections*. In the earlier novel, published in 1981, Karen twice speaks for many women torn between family and career. Her conversations, one with Bliss, a second with Wren, are interesting. A lifelong small-town homemaker, Bliss has difficulty understanding Karen's motivations, her needs for a life in the big city with its excitement and cocktail parties and glitter and glitz. Wren, her adult life ahead of her, is both more curious and detached when Karen tries to explain the attractions of Atlanta and Chicago. Wren even wonders if her own life with Sam will have these pushes and pulls as she tries to balance a role at home with a life as a concert pianist. Karen ends her talk with Wren with an echo of the Robert Frost poem "The Road Not Taken": "It was as if there were two roads and one of them looked so familiar, so ordinary. I just had to take the other one. I had to" (210).

Karen's behavior bothered Bridgers, still does. What ought she to do? What options does she have? Here is Bridgers on Karen:

> I especially like Karen because I have worried about her so much. I didn't want her to be misinterpreted; so I tried very hard to make her true to herself, to do what was necessary for herself so that she could make a life despite how people felt about her leaving her family. I didn't want to think about whether she was right or wrong in leaving. I was determined not to judge her. I wanted instead to accept the fact that she said to me, "This is what I have to do. This is my survival." It was as if a friend had said that to me. The kind of support I would give a friend, I had to give to Karen. . . . I never wanted to be judgmental. I just wanted to present the facts of a life.[15]

In *Permanent Connections* Ginny Collier reflects often on her own failed marriage. She likens it to Coralee's need for protection:

> "I've got to stay safe," Coralee said stubbornly.
> "I thought that, too," Ginny said. "I married because of it. I did everything I was told because of it. But in the long run being safe meant being in prison."
> "I'm afraid. Sometimes when I'm lying in bed, my breathing stops I'm so scared," Coralee said. "I think I'm scared of dying more than anything."
> "Maybe so," Ginny said, "but my problem was that I was afraid to live." (134)

Two women, then, Karen and Ginny, the one trapped in a small town away from the big city and the corporate life she wants, the other trapped in a big city and a failed marriage away from the rural independence she wants: both offer significant commentary on the role of women, just as do, in their own ways, Stella and Maggie, Jane and Pansy, Bliss, Sara Will. The significance of women, in her life and in her novels, never strays far from Bridgers's consciousness.

These themes—love, family harmony and disharmony, mental illness, connections, the intervention of the outsider, the role of women—constitute the major themes in Bridgers's writing. Their presence and her thoughtful commentary on them suggest that Bridgers may focus on ideas even more than she realizes.

5. The Significance of Setting

Sue Ellen Bridgers lives in a small Southern town. And small Southern towns live in her novels and stories. Other authors have created regions and used them as settings for several works: Faulkner's Yoknatawpha County is home base for a number of his novels, for example.

But few novelists who write for young adults have so centered their work in a particular locale as Bridgers has done. Her stage is rural North Carolina, several hours from big urban sprawls like Charlotte or even bigger ones like Atlanta, places that, though they are reachable, are really "special occasion" cities. Her characters know of such places, indeed may work there, as does Karen in *Notes for Another Life*, but most of her people live out their lives in their small towns, generally not far from where they were born and reared.

Bridgers's South: Fact and Fiction

The small towns Bridgers describes so well are, for the most part, safe places, havens where people talk about you when you are well, but take care of you when you are sick. Erroneously viewed by Northerners in "Yankee Country" as gossipy little backwaters where nothing ever happens, in fact life in the small towns Bridgers creates is rich and complex and, further, is private unless and until some unusual event makes it part of the public domain. You can leave the back door unlatched when you go to bed. If your car will not start on a winter morning—and cold, wintry, sometimes even snowy mornings do exist each year—you'll know who your neighbor is and that he will give you a lift to work, from where you can call the filling station (seldom the "service station"), tell them about the car, and be confident that all will be well by the time you return home that evening. When the kitchen sink springs a leak, chances are good you will be able to call the plumber by first name—if not when he arrives, certainly by the time he leaves.

Small? Yes. Rural? Certainly. But uneventful? Yes, compared with the earth-changing actions that can occur in Washington, D.C., or Moscow, but not when judged on their own merits. As Bridgers says, "the rural way of life is not necessarily a simple way of life. Although the setting of my books is rural and big adventurous things don't happen, the internal lives of people there can be very complicated. What they decide to do about their lives is just as important at the moment as when some powerful person is going through a big emotional upheaval. For rural people to be considered simple is really pejorative."[1]

Relatives—kinfolk—signify in small Southern towns. Typically one has aunts and uncles, cousins and in-laws networking throughout the streets and alleys. Great Aunt Marge lives down the street with her son, cousin Evan, and the city wife he found when he was in the service and whom it will take a while to get real fond of. In the house next door where she and Marge were born, lives Ida, an old maid who is surrogate mother to her many nieces and nephews and a sure bet for a piece of fudge or a freshly baked cookie. Bridgers writes of exactly this awareness of her relatives in her own upbringing:

> The house my parents built, and into which we moved when I was six, was beside Grandmother's. Ma's [Her other grandmother] house was perhaps a half-mile away, on the other end of Winterville, an easy walk. One block over from us lived Ma's

sister, my great-aunt Dora, in the house their father had built
in 1880. Out in the country three miles from Winterville was
Renston where Grandmother had grown up. . . . We were surrounded by kin.[2]

It is this kind of small Southern town in which Sue Ellen Bridgers was reared, and her roots and her clear attachment to them
inform virtually every page of her fiction. Yet, curiously, she often
introduces an outsider into these environs and through him or
her carries on much of the description of what life is like in rural
Carolina. Typically, too, the outsider is forced by circumstance or
parental dictate rather than personal intent to move to the country.

Though it was his own home years earlier, the back country
to which James Earl returns in *Home before Dark* is clearly
alien territory for Stella, who loves it, and her mother Mae, who
hates it.

Casey comes unwillingly to the small town where Dwayne lives,
a town Bridgers herself depicts as "one of the central characters
in *All Together Now*."[3] True, Casey has been there before, but
only for short visits; now she is to spend the summer. And "she
wished she hadn't come" (5).

In *Sara Will* Fate and Eva join Sara Will and Swanee Hope to
find sanctuary away from Eva's searching parents. Fate calls
Tyler Mills "the sticks" and indeed it is. Yet that is why Fate had
selected it as offering Eva the hiding place she needed.

Big-city boy Rob, born and raised in New Jersey, initially finds
almost no attractions in his father's homeplace near Tyler Mills
in *Permanent Connections*, nor does Ellery, newly arrived from
Charlotte. Early in their relationship Ellery tells Rob about Tyler
Mills: "You will find, as a visitor from worlds beyond, that the
resources of this planet are quite limited, as in nonexistent" (38).
When Rob learns that he must stay in the country to care for
Uncle Fairlee, Aunt Coralee, and his grandfather, it is the locale
that enrages him as much as the assignment.

But in every instance, save Mae's, these outsiders come to sense
in their new homeplace its appeal, not only to its residents (usu-

ally their relatives) but also to them. Values of the small towns become their values. The rural way of life becomes their way of life. Bridgers's skill in portraying village Carolina in a way that makes the conversion of the outsiders believable merits attention.

Most novelists who write for teenage audiences tread lightly on what their readers might term excessive description; they show, rather than tell. Bridgers uses the same methods, enabling readers to learn about the areas where her characters live by their actions and their own observations about their surroundings. Almost at first meeting James Earl is shown to be a man of the South: On the Willises' way back to North Carolina from their migrant life he has stopped to buy the family a typical "meal"— four different kinds of candy and crackers for Mae and the children and "a bag of peanuts that he poured into his own Pepsi bottle" (6). Northerners may eat peanuts with their soft drinks, but they don't pour them into the bottle. Other southerners do. Observe the young Osborn boy in *The Whisper of the River* by Ferrol Sams: "Porter poured a nickel bag of Planter's peanuts into his Coca-Cola bottle and chewed and drank rapidly."[4] Rob's grandfather Dickson names his children after Southern heroes in the Civil War: Fairlee, Coralee, and Rosalie after General Robert E. Lee and Rob's father Davis after Confederate President Jefferson Davis. At mealtime beans, cornbread, and fried okra complement an entree in a Bridgers novel.

Bridgers can describe in powerful ways. Though it is Rodney who has taken Stella to the tobacco auction in *Home before Dark*, it is Toby's sensibilities that permit it to be shared with the reader, almost palpably:

> Toby could tell Stella how it felt to step on mice and feel the soft infant bodies rolling under his boot until the floor was bloody and raw. Or how the sky looked on nights when he lay in a tobacco truck under the stars, not because Newton needed him to watch the barns but because he wanted the feeling of being completely alone, just Toby Brown and the barn owls and the old cat sleeping at his feet and so many stars the sky seemed on fire. (42–43)

Just as Toby wants to be Stella's tour guide and help her sense, feel, almost ingest the atmosphere of the tobacco warehouse, so also does Bridgers convey the same impression—she wants us to be there. It is obviously a special place to her, one she recalls from her own youth and her father's work as a tobacco farmer. Only someone who has actually been there, like Toby or Bridgers, can provide that kind of description; Rodney would be at best superficial, at worst false.

In two of her novels—*Sara Will* and *Permanent Connections*—Bridgers provides a name for the small town of her setting—Tyler Mills. The other novels are also set in what clearly is a Tyler Mills type of town, here described, albeit too harshly, by Fate in *Sara Will*: "Tyler Mills. He could see the bleak little town, one straight narrow street of brick storefronts, their canvas awnings rolled up like eyelids over vacant eyes" (52).

The Tyler Mills Fate returns to is changed somewhat from the one he recalls. It now has a steakhouse to which Eva, Swanee Hope, and Sara Will go one evening for a night out while Fate and Michael are at its new bowling alley. When Rob and Ellery comment on its nothingness, they do so at Ennis's, a hamburger drive-in. As Ellery tells Rob, there is even "Bert's Service Center, where, on odd nights—e.g., when there's a full moon or an electrical storm, both occasions when respectable folks are not abroad—you can buy bootleg beer, even a pint of something akin to gin. This is a dry county, you see" (38). The town in *All Together Now* has a lumberyard that Ben owns and a dime store where Gwen works and a movie theater where Casey and Dwayne watch the Saturday serializations common in 1951. It also has a dirt track where Taylor races his green Mercury. Bill owns a drugstore in *Notes for Another Life* and, in *Home before Dark*, James Earl takes over Maggie Grover's general store after their marriage.

So much then for the towns, the places, in Bridgers's novels. Attention to her settings must also include the households, their furnishings, their memories, the piano that Bliss and Wren love in *Notes for Another Life*, the tenant shack that Stella paints and, by so doing, converts a house into a home in *Home before Dark*, the kitchen from which the agoraphobic Coralee cannot escape in *Permanent Connections*. Bridgers describes these all with a clear vision that translates into image-producing prose. A reader can see the great room in the house Ginny herself designed in *Permanent Connections*, where she weaves at her loom, and the dining room in *All Together Now*, where Gwen toys with her shrimp and shad because she cannot eat seafood but does not want to offend Jane, whom she hopes to have as a mother-in-law. It is this same dining room where Hazard causes all forks to pause in midair because he proposes to Pansy and she accepts.

Bridgers did not have to create these rooms out of the whole cloth of imagination. She had spent numerous childhood hours in just such houses, the one in which she was reared and her grandmothers' houses nearby. She provides her own invitation to visit:

> Come in. The hall is cool, but with sunlight at the back like an airy, fragrant tunnel. Come into the parlor, the dining room. See the screen door through which food miraculously appears as mother brings platters on her arms for Sunday dinner or company supper. There is the stairway where children huddle in the dark listening to the talk below. . . . Above and below are bedrooms, and also the spare room for the loom and the desk at which grandmother kept accounts. Further below the cool cellar where sweet potatoes, Irish potatoes, cabbages, and apples breathe the dirt and endure.
>
> This is a homeplace. It is set in a field as if it is a rare and wonderful plant cultivated by a woman's care and formed to her design.[5]

Southern Life: Fact and Fiction

These rooms in these houses in these towns in North Carolina exist in fact as well as in Bridgers's fiction. Life in these places may be different from what it is elsewhere, though not always in the ways people outside the South expect. The South's summer heat and humidity slow the movement of the population, but winter chills and their occasional accompanying snowfalls quicken it so that, on balance, the pace of life in the South is about what it is everywhere else. What is different is that people in the South *seem* to have more time, at least to take more time. The "have a nice day" expression that ubiquitously ends every transaction from buying a house to paying for a hamburger takes on an altered meaning in the South. It is not a mindless utterance. People there seem willing to spend the moment to give it meaning; they are serious about wishing you a nice day.

In Sylva, where Bridgers lives, the stunning beauty of the nearby Great Smoky Mountains may give pause to motion, too. Springtime dogwoods and azaleas and dazzling autumn colors contribute to a slowing down. Who wants to hurry when such beauty exists right outside the front door? The advice of the apocryphal South Alabama philosopher—"Take time to smell the flowers"—is heeded in the country Bridgers writes about. James Earl fingers with genuine love the tobacco-growing earth in *Home before Dark*. Ginny regularly marvels at the changing beauty of the mountains that surround her home in *Permanent Connections*.

Talk differs in these places, too, though again in ways not suggested by the conventional wisdom. Linguists who engage in word counting like to shatter the myth of the Southern drawl. Southerners actually speak faster than Northerners, they report, proving their assertions with taped recordings of speech. Bridgers herself speaks very rapidly and reads the speeches she gives in part to have some idea of the time they will take, in part to avoid speech that is too rapid. But there is no denying that there is something that can be called a Southern dialect. People in the South do use different terms and different pronunciations for a few common items. Fried eggs (sometimes "aigs") that are greaSy in the North are greaZy in the South. Bridgers describes an area near Sylva called a "holler," only partly because it is in a valleylike hollow; the people there, almost all kin, can "holler" to each other. A young woman she knew greatly outstripped her parents' rather modest ambitions for her, then somewhat turned her back on these parents. She was guilty of "risin' above her raisin'."

Yet Bridgers does not include many examples of regional dialects in her books. No one fries breakfast in a "spider" (Southern for *skillet* or *frying pan*). Bliss does not "carry" (Southern for *take*) Wren to the asylum to visit Tom in *Notes for Another Life*. In *Permanent Connections* Fairlee and Rob's grandfather occasionally lapse into regional speech, but for the most part Bridgers's characters speak the way they would if they lived in New England or California. And that is exactly how she should portray them. The truth is that most Southern speech is like most Northern or Eastern or Western speech in syntax, in word choice, in pronunciation. To create a character whose "y'all's" or "honey chile's" covered the pages like some smothering kudzu plant would detract from the universality she hopes her characters will have.

What their speech suggests is that, first and foremost, Bridgers's characters are real people, universal. She places them in the rural South because that is the area she knows best, one she loves. This knowledge and love facilitate her picturing it in honest, accurate, and affectionate ways.

Bridgers is herself Southern. Her speech has that softness, that false sense of slowness, one associates with the South. She extols the South as a place to live, to raise a family. She likes its small towns. To be sure, there are the rotters, like the overly zealous policeman in *Permanent Connections* and the immature Rodney Biggers in *Home before Dark*. But generally the towns are good places for her characters to spend their lives in, for Bridgers herself to live in. Though she is indeed a sophisticated woman, at home in the bustling Atlanta airport she frequently has to use to travel to her many speaking engagements, comfortable with a glass of chilled Chardonnay at a publisher's soiree in midtown Manhattan, as a writer she remembers her roots. And honors them.

6. Conclusion

Hillaire Belloc once said, "Of all the fatiguing, futile, empty trades, the worst, I suppose, is writing about writing." But perhaps not, when the subject is as skilled an author as Sue Ellen Bridgers, though she herself comments that "writing" is "something better accomplished than talked about."[1] As these chapters have attempted to indicate, Bridgers tells good stories about interesting characters with significant problems. It remains to look more closely at her particular writing strengths and weaknesses and to place her work in context in young adult literature and also in contemporary Southern regional literature.

Writing Style

Style is that most elusive of literary qualities, difficult to define, almost impossible to agree on. Voltaire allowed that "every style that is not boring is a good one." Katherine Anne Porter said, "I've been called a stylist until I really could tear my hair out. And I simply don't believe in style. The style is you." But George Bernard Shaw believed in style, calling it "the effectiveness of assertion. He who has nothing to assert has no style and can have none." Truman Capote was even more vehement: "There is such an animal as a nonstylist, only they're not writers—they're typists."

Bridgers clearly has something to assert and clearly she does much more than merely type. As these pages have revealed, she excels in a number of writing tasks that help define a writer's style—character development, plot structure, thematic treatment, the use of setting.

Other criteria about style, however, may usefully be examined as they apply to Bridgers's works. One such standard is clarity. Can her works be understood? A writer who presumes to write for a young adult audience must, perhaps above all other things, be clear. If she cannot be easily understood, she will not be easily—or often—read. In that criterion lies a difficulty that besets the educator who attempts to teach Shakespeare to teenagers: the students may not understand what they are asked to read. Thus, a teacher's job with a Shakespearean play is to make the unclear clear. But a young adult author like Bridgers will be more commonly read by teenagers on their own. If, as often occurs, her work is assigned in a classroom setting, a teacher can confidently say to students, "Read," and know that they will understand what Bridgers is saying. Not for her the oblique phrase, the obscure symbol. She does often write in metaphors, but they are accessible metaphors, exactly the kind a writer must choose if she is to appeal to teenagers whose reading sophistication is still being shaped, who are still better able to handle the literal than to fathom the sublime. Possibly even without being aware of it, she takes as a guiding principle this dictum from Stendhal: "I see but one rule: *to be clear*. If I am not clear, all my world crumbles to nothing."

Another criterion of style may be found in the artistry of the details a writer presents to her readers. Such details are the little pieces of writing—the apt word, the perfect phrase or clause, the vivid image or metaphor, the absolutely right conversational response. They are the lines a reader pauses over, reads again, takes delight in for their own sake. Their skillful use moves a good storyteller to the ranks of gifted writers, an accolade Bridgers deserves because of her ability with these details. For example, early in *Permanent Connections* she gives a capsule description of Rob Dickson, not by telling about *him*, but by letting him think of a writing assignment he is reluctant to do: "Right now he should get up and write something. He would write about how it feels when you wake up in the night because your folks are arguing about you, about how lousy it is never to be left alone, about what a pain in the butt your twelve year old perfect sister is, about how you're already messed up. Already, at seventeen, boxed in with no way out. Not enough guts to scramble, never enough bucks to float. Sinking, always sinking. Holding tight and falling away at the same time" (6).

In that same book Ellery tries to explain to Rob her passion for fine music: "There are twelve notes in a scale. With the same twelve notes, Beethoven wrote nine symphonies, Mozart wrote *Eine Kleine Nachtmusik*, Vivaldi wrote the Four Seasons. Surely you'll admit they did more with twelve notes than Michael Jackson ever has" (84).

The author of those compelling lines gave promise early in her career of a signal capacity with details. In her first novel *Home before Dark* Bridgers wrote of the Willis family's migrant life: "They seemed to have existed just because living was there to do, not because there was any joy in it" (126). The death of Mae in the tobacco barn in that novel is a slowly moving portrait in words that appeal to all of a reader's senses; one can almost see the lightning flash, hear the roar of the thunder, feel the electricity in the air, smell the flesh burning, taste the bile in Toby's mouth when he discovers the stricken Mae.

In *Notes for Another Life* Bridgers provides in a passage of fewer than seventy words a memorable summary of Bliss's active life and a reminder that Tom's condition is never far from her consciousness: "Bliss thought, I've lived at least three fourths of my life, I've taught at least ten thousand hours of piano lessons, cooked and cleaned, spent considerable time in church, on the tennis court, and at club meetings, none of which matter very much. What mattered was Tom, her failure. Her silent, spiritually paralyzed child who had found some sinister, odious kind of deliverance in his private madness" (40).

Details abound in *All Together Now*. Pansy is pleased about the marriage to Hazard, knowing that it is time she married: "She was not, after all, old wine; more likely, a spice that could lose its savor" (101). And, if not an out-and-out loser, surely not one of life's winners, Hazard at last realizes that he has done something correctly: "Loving Pansy was the most right thing he had ever done" (140).

Most of Bridgers's details offer this same compactness, this ability to say a lot in a little space with, typically, the absolutely best words to do that job. As Mark Twain said, "The difference between the right word and the almost right word is the difference between lightning and the lightning bug." Bridgers almost always writes lightning, with sentence after sentence, paragraph after paragraph, using, to quote Twain again, "just the right words, not their second cousins."

Yet her writing may be criticized on a few counts. To portray characters, to tell the readers what they look like, plagues many writers, Bridgers included. Textbooks on fiction seem to suggest that characters should be revealed by what they say and do and by what others say about them. Still, these revelations are words put on the page by the author, who may want to provide some more description, some straightforward "Harold was tall, big-boned, with shirts that seemed tailored for an even larger man so that it appeared he could almost turn around inside them." Unfortunately, rather than simply describe her characters in expository sentences, Bridgers tends to overuse a single device to assist her in character descriptions—a conveniently located mirror.

This habit, one of only minor annoyance but bothersome still, seems most evident in *Sara Will*. In her fifties with, so one can imagine, many years in front of her bureau mirror Sara Will nonetheless "moved closer to the mirror, looking at herself as if for the first time" (60). She studies her face again at that same mirror just a few pages later. Michael "stopped in front of the small mirror just to look at himself" (95). Eva shares the communal narcissism and initiates infant Rachel: "She stood up in the bathroom, the baby against her chest, and looked at the two of them in the mirror" (103).

In *Notes for Another Life* Kevin is the mirror watcher: After a shower "he brought the towel to the mirror. In two quick swipes he could see himself . . . a gaunt face, hollow, meatless" (47). After his recovery from the suicide attempt and his subsequent decision that life is worth living, he examines himself once more: "The face he saw looked different, the mouth lines somehow softer, the eyes more direct" (225).

To focus on this kind of trivial writing lapse borders on the ungenerous. After all, even when Bridgers locates her characters' introspection near a handy mirror, their judgments about themselves add to the understanding readers have of them. Yet, given her use of omniscience as her author's perspective, Bridgers clearly could and should have varied the strategies she employed to reveal her characters' features. Wren could notice that brother Kevin's face seemed thoughtful; Eva could judge the weakness in Michael's chin.

This minor sin aside, questions still must be raised about a more serious criticism, one that has surfaced on occasion among Bridgers's reviewers: the charge of sentimentality. In their *Handbook to Literature* literary scholars Thrall and Hibbard define "sentimentality" as "an overindulgence in emotion, especially the conscious effort to induce emotion."[2] Robert C. Small, Jr., wrote that *Notes for Another Life* is "flawed by a sentimental tone."[3] After praising the novels Bridgers had written for adolescents (*Home before Dark, All Together Now*, and *Notes for Another Life*), Alice Digilio said about *Sara Will*: "Her toughness has always been softened by sentiment. Now . . . it's apparent that Bridgers's sentiment, unchecked and uncontrolled, fast becomes sentimentality."[4] It is a concern Bridgers takes seriously and about which she answers forthrightly: "Being sentimental scares me. Yet I think reviewers call things sentimental that are just ordinary experiences. If it's not a high flung happening and if it doesn't involve the Holocaust or life and death, then it's sentimental. Too, small towns and appearing to be sentimental seem to go together for some critics."[5]

What of this charge and Bridgers's reaction to it? Clearly she does come nearer the edge of sentimentality in the novels criticized above than in her others. Sara Will's difficulties with Swanee Hope and her vacillating introspection about Fate's advances tend to get a bit cloying. A reader might be tempted to say, "Get on with it." C. B. Jenkins ended his review with this pungent assertion:

> When Sara Will has the garden plowed, two pages before the novel's close, the author's elbow insistently nudges the reader's ribs as Sara thinks, "Everything changes . . . even me. To plant a seed the ground must be disturbed, a surface altered." A touch more disorder, for Bridgers as well as Sara Will, might have better tested everyone's moral fiber while taking the didactic lecture off these lessons.[6]

In *Notes for Another Life* Bridgers tugs at the heartstrings perhaps more than she should. To be sure, Kevin is a victim, but his persistent self-pity and Bridgers's apparent tolerance for it seem manipulative. Even less real is the characterization of Wren, whose sweetness at first simply surfaces, then surfeits. More nearly perfect than she should be, she needs the spunk of a Stella, the anger of a Casey, the fire of an Ellery before she can completely capture a reader's concern.

Yet even in these novels any charge of sentimentality must be leavened with the totality of the experiences recorded. If at times Kevin seems overdrawn, Wren too sweet, Sara Will too much the curmudgeon whose heart of gold will be revealed at novel's end, on balance their characterizations ring true, reveal real people with problems that demand and get real emotional reactions from readers. It could be, too, that Bridgers suffers from her own early success. No grumbles about sentimentality accompanied either *Home before Dark* or *All Together Now*, nor would any have stuck. The characters in those novels, their situations, their triumphs and failures are the stuff of well-wrought fiction, a kind of consummate artistry Bridgers returned to in *Permanent Connections*. That she slipped a tad in the books written between them may be forgiven.

Bridgers and the Young Adult Novel

Novelists come in many shapes and sizes and with many different philosophies and styles, not just novelists in general but also those categorized in certain ways—mystery authors, science fiction writers, young adult novelists. Within the categories are broad ranges. Yet such classifications have their uses, tending more to describe than to delimit. Readers can expect certain directions, themes, characters, plot devices, perhaps even settings. Sue Ellen Bridgers, however, often defies the predictions readers can make about young adult novelists and thus both departs from and broadens the category.

That the novel will be principally about an adolescent character may be the most supportable generalization of all in the field of young adult literature. From Fran Arrick to Paul Zindel, Robert Cormier to S. E. Hinton to Norma Fox Mazer, writers for young adults write about young adults, if not exclusively then primarily. But not Bridgers. Certainly her four novels intended for adolescents (if not always by her, then by her critics, by teachers, librarians, and teenage readers) all have central characters who are young adults, and even the adult novel *Sara Will* has Eva and Michael, both teenagers. In none of these novels, however, do these teenagers command the whole stage. In *Home before Dark* James Earl and, first Mae, then Maggie, have stories that must be told. Jane and Ben, Pansy and Hazard, Gwen and Taylor, and especially Dwayne are central to *All Together Now*; adolescent Casey is the pivot point. Sixty-two-year-old Bliss occupies the protagonist's role in *Notes for Another Life* almost as fully as Wren or Kevin; Karen and Tom also play important parts. Bridgers comes closer to the generalization in *Permanent Connections* than in any of her other works, but even in this work other, older characters—Ginny, Coralee, Fairlee—are fully described, with problems that are woven, like the threads in Ginny's loom, into the entire fabric of the novel.

This large catalog of characters, many of them well beyond adolescent years, derives from Bridgers's considerable desire and significant ability to get to know all her characters well, the adolescents, the older women, the minor characters. The common perspective in young adult fiction is first-person narration, a technique that more often than not limits the author to one character throughout the work. Bridgers allows no such restriction and moves smoothly from one character to another, from one age to another.

Because most young adult novels are about teenagers and because schooling is the chief vocational activity of people this age, it is to be expected that a novel for adolescents will give some attention to schools and teachers, homework and grades. Zindel, for example, offers ten guidelines that he tries to follow in his novels, the first of which is "Stories should relate in part to school environments since this is where teenagers spend most of their time."[7] Not so in a Bridgers novel. Though Stella, Toby, and Rodney Biggers all go to school in *Home before Dark*, it seems to play almost no part in their lives. Casey in *All Together Now* is on summer vacation, the time frame for a large part of both *Notes for Another Life* and *Permanent Connections*. It is true that in *Permanent Connections* Rob, Ellery, Leanna, and Travis attend school and a few scenes are set there, but rarely does it serve as a catalyst for action in the manner it does in novels of other writers for young adults. In *Sara Will* Eva drops out of school when she discovers her pregnancy. Michael has graduated and goes on to junior college, but his experiences in the classroom are barely hinted at.

Neither Bridgers's lack of knowledge about schools nor any lack of interest in them causes this omission in her writing. She simply chooses to write about other matters. Education is important to her and to her family. She did well in school herself and later in college, both before her marriage to Ben and later when she returned to the university after her children had grown; in fact, she graduated with highest honors. Too, she and Ben have gone to considerable lengths to educate their own children, sending them first to boarding schools for their secondary education and to private colleges for higher education. Her decision to exclude much attention to schooling from her writing thus is just that— an author's decision.

Sex plays a significant role in the novels of many writers for teenagers. Zindel again: "Romance and the characters' awkward attempts at it should be incorporated into the stories."[8] Only in *Permanent Connections* are the attempts, awkward or otherwise, made in Bridgers's work. Rob and Ellery have sex, at which both are apparently experienced though hardly promiscuous. In her other novels for teenagers sex plays almost no part at all. Even in the adult novel *Sara Will* in which Eva has had one instance of sex, passionless but consequential—she conceives Rachel—and Fate and Sara celebrate their mid-life marriage, sex itself receives almost Victorian treatment, only occasionally referred to and, then, obliquely.

Not uncommonly in novels for adolescents adults are portrayed as stupid or ineffectual or even downright venal. Zindel's fictional parents are often borderline psychotics. Hinton's are usually absent from the central scenes of her novels. Cormier's adults seem to exercise either little or malign influence on the young around them. Many other writers for young adults follow similar patterns in characterizing adults. Bridgers again forges her own way, however, creating fully fleshed adults—often belonging to an older generation—of civility, intelligence, and compassion. Rarely is an adult the villain of the piece, as is the policeman who arrests Rob in *Permanent Connections*. More typically the adult characters share the same goals and values the teenagers have. The adults often assume responsibility for shaping these goals and values. Even a minor figure like Gwen in *All Together Now* takes it upon herself to instruct Casey in the ways of romance: "Don't ever make a person you care about have to choose between you and something else" (175).

Given, then, Bridgers's rejection of the standard, not to say stereotypical, aspects of the young adult novel, ought she to be considered a novelist for adolescents? She herself voices reservations:

> Having come to young adult literature without scholarship or experience, I find I have ambivalent feelings about such a classification. I am not sure there needs to be a category of young adult literature at all, and I don't understand the criteria for its classification. If it means that, because of their style or subject matter, beautifully written, accomplished stories that stretch the reader's understanding of life are eliminated, then I hope young adult literature as a category dies quickly. If it means that young people are given access to good books that might otherwise go unpublished for lack of a market, then I have warm wishes for its future.
>
> . . . One thing I know for certain. Young people deserve the best the community of writers has to offer.[9]

Yet a central question remains, Who reads her novels? Adolescents do. She is popular in schools, where her books are often read as classroom requirements. Both school and public libraries stock and promote her writing, frequently in young adult sections. She reports a steady flow of mail from teenage readers, which she answers, and positive responses from the teenage members of the many audiences she addresses. Finally, she has become the subject of many articles and convention presentations on adolescents' literature.

What this popularity suggests is that the generalizations about young adult literature may be faulty. Oliver Wendell Holmes said it: "No generalization is worth a damn—including this one." Including those about teenage novels. Bridgers merits a place in the field of fiction for young adults because that is where she finds her most consistent and appreciative readers.

Bridgers as a Southern Writer

Beyond her legitimacy as a writer for young adults is another category of writers to which Bridgers belongs: the contemporary

Southern writer. All of Bridgers's work is set in the South, more specifically in the small towns of North Carolina, and in this regard she joins a number of other contemporary writers who see the South as the proper locale for their literary endeavors. Novelists as serious as Anne Rivers Siddons or Wilma Dykeman, as humorous as Clyde Edgerton or Ferrol Sams, as contemporary as Lee Smith or as nostalgic as Olive Burns, place their stories in the South. Yet Bridgers has more in common with these writers than the shared setting.

When asked about contemporary writers whom she admires, Bridgers quickly responds with the name of Anne Tyler. Like Bridgers, Tyler clearly seems far more interested in character than in plot. Moreover, her characters play their parts on a small stage. They seldom engage in cataclysmic events that will change the world. Almost always they interact with families, often vertical families. And Tyler sets her novels in the South. The city of Baltimore, often the place of residence of her characters, is a Southern city in Tyler's hands. Some of her novels are actually set in North Carolina. Tyler's *If Morning Ever Comes* begins in New York, but in its opening pages drifting law school student Ben Joe Hawkes returns to Sandhill, North Carolina, and his six sisters, his widowed mother, his paternal grandmother. Once there, Ben Joe begins to understand his own uncertainty about himself. It is the stuff of his family, their denial of involvement, their reluctance even to admit that Ben Joe's father's blatant infidelity had any impact on their lives. They keep everything in.

Most Southern writers exhibit the passionate love for the South and its people that Bridgers includes in all of her writing. Clyde Edgerton's three novels are, like all of Bridgers's, set in North Carolina. And, like Bridgers's, they feature ordinary people, not presidents or international spies or even locally important folk. The elderly protagonist of *Walking across Egypt* would be at home with Bliss and Jane, sharing recipes and worries about their adult children. Raney, the central figure of the novel that bears her name, is every bit as Southern as Grandpa Dickson, whose greatest tragedy is that the South lost *the* war. The family dinners in *Raney* resemble those in *All Together Now* and *Notes for Another*

Life, right down to the discussions of this year's crop of black-eyed peas. Edgerton's *Floatplane Notebooks* demonstrates the same sort of extended family Bridgers often includes, only his goes back even further, spanning four generations and requiring a family tree in the front matter of the book. Anne Rivers Siddons titled one of her novels *Homeplace* and, in it, brought a long-absent daughter back from the city into the rural South. Her outsider, though an adult, creates some of the same catalytic energies that Bridgers's outsiders set loose.

Two other contemporary Southern writers explore adolescence, though, like Bridgers, their teenage characters are a part of the story, not the whole of it. Ferrol Sams's *Run with the Horsemen* and its sequel, *The Whisper of the River*, introduce Porter Osborn, Jr., a largely autobiographical creation patterned on Sams's own 1930s Georgia upbringing. Osborn, like Casey in *All Together Now* or Rob in *Permanent Connections* and like Bridgers when she was growing up, is surrounded by family—his mother, his many cousins, his grandmother who dips snuff. Also with more family than one teenager ought to have to handle is Will Tweedy, the young protagonist of Olive Ann Burns's *Cold Sassy Tree*. His grandfather, one-armed (like Fate Jessop in *Sara Will*), only three weeks a widower, has decided to remarry. His daughters are stunned but far from speechless. And young Will, as memorable a character as Stella or Casey, is front and center a part of his grandfather's plans. As in *All Together Now* this novel offers its readers a picture of an entire community.

This same event—a widowed father's plans to remarry and the way this news reverberates among his adult children—provides the plot line of another Southern novel, Peter Taylor's *Summons to Memphis*. Again, the focus with Taylor is on character, not on plot, and, again, families extend vertically as well as horizontally. The descriptions of their youth in, first, Nashville, then Memphis, provide almost vintage glimpses of what the South was like earlier in this century and, to some degree, still appears to be in the writings of many Southern authors.

Another of them, Reynolds Price (also a Bridgers favorite), places his many stories in the South, usually nearer North Carolina where Bridgers grew up. *A Long and Happy Life*, his first novel, actually featured adolescents caught in the same sorts of family webbings in which Bridgers often places her protagonists. Rosacoke Mustian, a teenager, is in love with Wesley Beavers, an ex-serviceman still in love with the surroundings—the girls—in Norfolk, where he was stationed. On one of his trips back home, only partly to see Rosacoke, they have their first actual sexual encounter and Rosacoke gets pregnant. Her worries about how and what to tell Wesley are complicated by her sister-in-law's pregnancy that ends in a stillbirth. Finally, she does tell Wesley, who shows a surprising sensitivity and urges their marriage. Price's title suggests that they may make it. Like Bridgers, Price describes the setting with great care and love. Readers can smell the woods where Rosacoke loves to go to search for deer, can see the edge-of-town park where the Baptist church holds its annual picnic, can hear the hymns at the Christmas pageant that provides a dramatic climactic scene for this award-winning novel.

There are numerous other Southern novelists writing today— Richard Marius, Bobbie Ann Mason, for example. These are people whose works Bridgers reads and with whom she may be favorably compared. Even these all too brief lines about just a few of their novels—Tyler and Price are especially prolific—reveal how they and Bridgers share more than a love for their Southern roots and settings. Almost all of them place character before plot. The family connections signify in their novels and the families are vertical. Parents and grandparents play active, shaping roles in the lives of their descendants, often more than age-mates. It is a rare Tyler novel that fails to devote at least a few pages to the rearing of its central characters, pages that imply the importance of older people in the lives of the young.

Adolescents are very much included in these vertical families. The several generations studied in Edgerton's *Floatplane Notebooks* feature teenagers in each stage. Readers learn a lot about young Phillip Carver and his sisters in Taylor's *Summons to Memphis*, their early rearing in Nashville, the disruptive move to Memphis, and their father's continual meddling in their lives. Their subsequent interference with his late-in-life marriage plans has a certain poetic justice. Rosacoke Mustian in Price's *Long and Happy Life* shows much the same determination Bridgers later gave Stella in *Home before Dark*.

But what Bridgers has most in common with these novelists and such esteemed Southern short story writers as Flannery O'Connor and Eudora Welty (two more of her favorite authors) is not setting or characters or plots but writing skill. Each of these authors differs from the other, just as each differs from Bridgers. Yet all of them have quotable sentences and paragraphs that virtually leap off the page, diamonds discovered in the coal black of print. All of them are fine, readable writers whose novels and stories merit the considerable critical acclaim they are getting. A student of literature may ask whether it stretches critical judgment to place a novelist like Bridgers who writes for adolescents among this gloried company of writers whose principal audiences are adult. One answer is that she belongs with them; she is as good as they. Perhaps, however, the best answer is that teenagers deserve their literary heroes, too. In Sue Ellen Bridgers they have one.

APPENDIX:
Bridgers's Honors and Prizes

Home before Dark

Best Books for Young Adults, 1976, American Library Association
Outstanding Children's Books of 1976, *New York Times*

All Together Now

Best Books for Young Adults, 1979, American Library Association
Boston Globe–Horn Book Award, 1979
Christopher Award, 1979
American Book Award Nominee, 1979

Notes for Another Life

Best Books for Young Adults, 1981, American Library Association
American Book Award Nominee, 1981

Sara Will

Best Books for Young Adults, 1985, American Library Association

Permanent Connections

Best Books for Young Adults, 1987, American Library Association
Gold Award from Parent's Choice, 1987

Notes and References

Page references from Bridgers's novels are taken from the original hardcover editions in all cases.

Chapter 1

1. *Something about the Author Autobiography Series*, vol. 1, ed. Adele Sarkissian (Detroit: Gale Research Co., 1984), 45; hereafter cited as *SAAS*.

2. Joseph Milner, "The Emergence of Awe in Recent Children's Literature," *Children's Literature* (New Haven: Yale University Press, 1982), 172.

3. *SAAS*, 47.

4. Interview with Ted Hipple, 5 November 1988.

5. "Stories My Grandmother Told Me, Part One," *ALAN Review*, Fall 1985, 44.

6. *SAAS*, 44–45.

7. Ibid., 47.

8. Ibid., 46.

9. "The World That Winter," *Crucible*, Spring 1971, 39–41.

10. "I Call This Place Mine," *Crucible*, Spring 1974, 34–39.

11. Ibid., 35.

12. "All Summer Dying," *Carolina Quarterly*, Spring 1972, 14–22.

13. "The Beginning of Something," in *Visions*, ed. Don Gallo (New York: Dell, 1987), 214–28.

14. Ibid., 227–28.

15. "Life's a Beach," in *Connections*, ed. Don Gallo (New York: Dell, 1989), 183–99.

Chapter 2

1. Mary K. Chelton, review of *Home before Dark, Westchester Library System Newsletter*, April 1977, 3.
2. Sheila Schwartz, review of *Home before Dark, ALAN Review*, Spring 1977, 21.
3. Lucy Milner, review of *Home before Dark, North Carolina English Teacher*, Fall 1978, 33.
4. Linda Bachelder et al., "Looking Backward: Trying to Find the Classic Young Adult Novel," *English Journal*, September 1980, 89.
5. *SAAS*, 47.
6. K. M. Flanagan, review of *All Together Now, Horn Book*, April 1979, 197.
7. Review of *All Together Now, Booklist*, September 1979, 1152.
8. Review of *All Together Now, Publisher's Weekly*, 5 March 1979, 105.
9. Katherine Paterson, review of *All Together Now, Washington Post Book World*, 13 May 1979, 3.
10. Sara Miller, review of *All Together Now, School Library Journal*, May 1979, 70.
11. Paterson, *Washington Post Book World*, 13 May 1979, 3.
12. Robert C. Small, review of *Notes for Another Life, ALAN Review*, Spring 1982, 25.
13. Jean Fritz, review of *Notes for Another Life, New York Times Book Review*, 15 November 1981, 56–58.
14. Janet French, review of *Notes for Another Life, School Library Journal*, September 1981, 133.
15. Joan Atkinson and Roger Sutton, "Letters," *School Library Journal*, January 1982, 57–58.
16. Dick Abrahamson, "Old Friends with New Titles," *English Journal*, September 1981, 75.
17. A. A. Flowers, review of *Notes for Another Life, Horn Book*, December 1981, 667.
18. Joan Atkinson, review of *Notes for Another Life, Voice of Youth Advocates (VOYA)*, October 1981, 20.
19. Fritz, *New York Times Book Review*, 15 November 1981.
20. Dannye Romine, review of *Sara Will, Charlotte Observer*, 7 April 1985, 9F.
21. Jeanne Buckley, review of *Sara Will, Library Journal*, January 1985, 82.
22. Mary K. Chelton, review of *Sara Will, VOYA*, December 1985, 318.
23. Ibid.

24. Alice Digilio, review of *Sara Will, Washington Post Book World,* 16 February 1985, C9.

25. Barbara Chatton, review of *Permanent Connections, School Library Journal,* March 1937, 168.

26. Ted Hipple, review of *Permanent Connections, ALAN Review,* Spring 1987, 27.

27. Review of *Permanent Connections, English Journal,* October 1987, 97.

28. Review of *Permanent Connections, Bulletin of the Center for Children's Books,* March 1987, 122.

29. Bettye Cannon, review of *Permanent Connections, Los Angeles Times Book Review,* 12 October 1987, 21.

30. Hazel Rochman, review of *Permanent Connections, New York Times Book Review,* 26 July 1987, 21.

31. Review of *Permanent Connections, Booklist,* 15 February 1987, 892.

32. Hipple interview.

33. Ibid.

34. Ibid.

35. Ibid.

Chapter 3

1. "No More Tears," unpublished speech, n.d.

2. "The Wisdom of Fiction," unpublished speech, n.d.

3. "Stories My Grandmother Told Me, Part Two," *ALAN Review,* Winter 1986, 55.

4. Anthony L. Manna and Sue Misheff, "Responding to the Magic: Sue Ellen Bridgers Talks about Writing," *ALAN Review,* Winter 1986, 57.

5. "The Wisdom of Fiction."

6. Hipple interview.

7. Review of *Home before Dark, Women in Libraries Newsletter,* March 1977, 21.

8. Betsy Lindau, review of *Home before Dark, Southern Pines Pilot,* 21 September 1977, 2–B.

9. Mignon Ballard, review of *All Together Now, Charlotte Observer,* 20 May 1979, 33.

10. Hipple interview.

11. Ibid.

12. Ibid.

13. "People, Families, and Mothers," *ALAN Review*, Fall 1981, 2.
14. Ibid.
15. "No More Tears."
16. Hipple interview.
17. Chatton, *School Library Journal*, March 1987, 87.
18. "Writing for My Life," unpublished speech, n.d.
19. Paterson, *Washington Post Book World*, 13 May 1979, 3.
20. "The Wisdom of Fiction."
21. "Writing for My Life."
22. Miller, *School Library Journal*, May 1979, 70.
23. "No More Tears."
24. Ibid.

Chapter 4

1. "No More Tears."
2. Ibid.
3. Hipple interview.
4. "No More Tears."
5. See reviews by Paterson, Small, Chatton.
6. "No More Tears."
7. "The Wisdom of Fiction."
8. Joseph Milner, in *Children's Literature*, 170.
9. Judith Guest, *The Mythic Family* (Minneapolis: Milkweed Editions, 1988), 2.
10. Hipple interview.
11. Ibid.
12. "No More Tears."
13. Hipple interview.
14. Ibid.
15. "No More Tears."

Chapter 5

1. Manna and Misheff, "Responding to the Magic," 56.
2. *SAAS*, 42.
3. Hipple interview.
4. Ferrol Sams, *The Whisper of the River* (Atlanta: Peachtree Press, 1984), 22.
5. "Stories My Grandmother Told Me, Part One."

Chapter 6

1. *SAAS*, 49.
2. W. F. Thrall and Addison Hibbard, *A Handbook to Literature* (New York: Odyssey Press, 1960), 451.
3. Small, *ALAN Review*, Spring 1982, 25.
4. Digilio, *Washington Post Book World*, 16 February 1985, C9.
5. Hipple interview.
6. C. B. Jenkins, review of *Sara Will*, *Greensboro Spectator*, 11 April 1985, 23.
7. Jack Jacob Forman, *Presenting Paul Zindel* (Boston: Twayne Publishers, 1988), 13–14.
8. Ibid.
9. In Kenneth L. Donelson and Alleen Pace Nilsen, *Literature for Today's Young Adults*, 3d ed. (Glenview, Ill.: Scott Foresman & Co., 1989), 197.

Selected Bibliography

Primary Works

Novels

All Together Now. New York: A. A. Knopf, 1979; paperback, Bantam, 1980.
Home before Dark. New York: A. A. Knopf, 1976; paperback, Bantam, 1977.
Notes for Another Life. New York: A. A. Knopf, 1981; paperback, Bantam, 1982.
Permanent Connections. New York: Harper & Row, 1987.
Sara Will. New York: Harper & Row, 1985.

Selected Stories

"All Summer Dying." *Carolina Quarterly*, Spring 1972, 14–22.
"The Beginning of Something." In *Visions*, edited by Don Gallo, 214–28. New York: Dell, 1987.
"Home before Dark." *Redbook*, July 1976.
"Life's a Beach." In *Connections*, edited by Don Gallo, 183–99. New York: Dell, 1990.
"Time and Love." *Cairn*, Spring 1975.
"The World That Winter." *Crucible.* Spring 1971, 39–41.

Articles

"People, Families, and Mothers." *ALAN Review*, Fall 1981, 1–4.
"Reader, Writer, Librarian—All Together Now." *North Carolina Libraries*, Winter 1979, 37–41.

"Stories My Grandmother Told Me, Part One." *ALAN Review*, Fall 1985, 44–47.
"Stories My Grandmother Told Me, Part Two." *ALAN Review*, Winter 1986, 53–55.
In *Something about the Author Autobiography Series*, vol. 1, edited by Adele Sarkissian, 39–52. Detroit: Gale Research Co., 1984.

Speeches

"No More Tears." Unpublished. Given to several different audiences.
"The Wisdom of Fiction." Unpublished. Given to several different audiences.
"Writing for My Life." Unpublished. Given to several different audiences.

Secondary Works

Books and Pamphlets

Carlsen, G. Robert, and Anne Sherrill. *Voices of Readers*. Urbana, Ill.: National Council of Teachers of English, 1988.
Cline, Ruth, and William McBride. *A Guide to Literature for Young Adults*. Glenview, Ill.: Scott Foresman & Co., 1983.
Donelson, Kenneth L., and Alleen Pace Nilsen. *Literature for Today's Young Adults*. 3d ed. Glenview, Ill.: Scott Foresman & Co., 1989.
Forman, Jack Jacob. *Presenting Paul Zindel*. Boston: Twayne Publishers, 1988.
Guest, Judith. *The Mythic Family*. Minneapolis: Milkweed Editions, 1988.
Hipple, Ted. *Teaching Adolescent Literature: A Guide*. New York: Bantam Books, 1985.
Probst, Robert. *Adolescent Literature: Response and Analysis*. Columbus: Merrill Publishing Company, 1984.
Reed, Arthea J. S. *Reaching Adolescents*. New York: Holt, Rinehart, & Winston, 1985.
Sams, Ferrol. *The Whisper of the River*. Atlanta: Peachtree Press, 1984.

Articles

Abrahamson, Dick. "Old Friends with New Titles." *English Journal*, September 1981, 75–77.

Batchelder, Linda; Patricia Kelly; Donald Kenney; and Robert Small. "Looking Backward: Trying to Find the Classic Young Adult Novel." *English Journal*, September 1980, 86–89.
Buswell, Lin. "Rural Youth: The Forgotten Minority." *ALAN Review*, Winter 1984, 12–15.
Hinson, Carolyn Mathews. "Appalachian Literature and the Adolescent Reader." *ALAN Review*, Fall 1983, 4–10.
Hipple, Ted, and Bruce Bartholomew. "The Novels College Freshmen Have Read." *ALAN Review*, Winter 1982, 8–11.
Hipple, Ted. "Sue Ellen Bridgers." In *Dictionary of Literary Biography, Volume 52. American Writers for Children since 1960: Fiction*, edited by Glenn E. Estes. Detroit: Gale Research Co., 1986.
Milner, Joseph. "The Emergence of Awe in Recent Children's Literature." In *Children's Literature*, 169–177. New Haven: Yale University Press, 1982.
Small, Robert C. "The South in Recent Young Adult Novels." *ALAN Review*, Winter 1986, 62–66.
Sutton, Roger. "The Critical Myth: Realistic YA Novels." *School Library Journal*, November 1982, 33–35.

Interviews

Ted Hipple interview with Sue Ellen Bridgers, Sylva, North Carolina, 5 November 1988.
Anthony L. Manna and Sue Misheff interview with Sue Ellen Bridgers, Detroit, November 1984. Published as "Responding to the Magic: Sue Ellen Bridgers Talks about Writing." *ALAN Review*, Winter 1986, 56–61.

Book Reviews

All Together Now
Ballard, Mignon. *Charlotte Observer*, 20 May 1979, 33.
Booklist, September 1979, 1152.
Clinton, D. G. *Christian Science Monitor*, 14 May 1979, B6.
Flanagan, K. M. *Horn Book*, April 1979, 197.
Journal of Reading, December 1979, 280.
Kirkus Reviews, 15 May 1979, 579.
Kruse, Martha. *VOYA*, June 1979, 21.
Miller, Sara. *School Library Journal*, May 1979, 70.
Paterson, Katherine. *Washington Post Book World*, 13 May 1979, 3.

110   PRESENTING SUE ELLEN BRIDGERS

Publisher's Weekly, 5 March 1979, 105.
Sucher, Mary. *ALAN Review*, Spring 1979, R–5.

Home before Dark
Bibliophile, April 1977, 9.
Chelton, M. K. *Westchester Library System Newsletter*, April 1977, 3.
Helfgott, Barbara. *New York Times Book Review*, 14 November 1976, 52.
Holtze, Sally Holmes. *Horn Book*, April 1977, 9.
Lindau, Betsy. *Southern Pines Pilot*, 21 September 1977, 2–B.
Milner, Lucy. *North Carolina English Teacher*, Fall 1978, 33.
Publisher's Weekly, 13 September 1976, 99.
Schwartz, Sheila. *ALAN Review*, Spring 1977, 21.
Women in Libraries Newsletter, March 1977, 21.

Notes for Another Life
Atkinson, Joan L. *School Library Journal*, January 1982, 57.
Atkinson, Joan L. *VOYA*, October 1981, 20
Burnette, Carol Winfrey. *Arts Journal*, December 1981, 27.
Flowers, A. A. *Horn Book*, December 1981, 667.
French, Janet. *School Library Journal*, September 1981, 133.
Fritz, Jean. *New York Times Book Review*, 15 November 1981, 56–58.
Greenlaw, M. Jean. *Journal of Reading*, February 1982, 486.
Horn Book, December 1981, 667.
Publisher's Weekly, 4 September 1981, 56.
Small, Robert C. *ALAN Review*, Spring 1982, 25.
Sutton, Roger. *School Library Journal*, January 1982, 57–58.

Permanent Connections
Booklist, 15 February 1987, 892.
Bulletin of the Center for Children's Books, March 1987, 122.
Cannon, Bettye. *Los Angeles Times Book Review*, 12 October 1987, 21.
Chatton, Barbara. *School Library Journal*, March 1987, 168.
English Journal, October 1987, 97.
Hipple, Ted. *ALAN Review*, Spring, 1987, 27.
Rochman, Hazel. *New York Times Book Review*, 26 July 1987, 21.
Twichell, Ethel R. *Horn Book*, May–June 1987, 346.
Youree, Beverly. *VOYA*, April 1987, 29.

Sara Will
Buckley, Jeanne. *Library Journal*, January 1985, 82–83.
Chelton, Mary K. *VOYA*, December 1985, 318.
Digilio, Alice. *Washington Post Book World*, 16 February 1985, C9.

Jenkins, C. B. *Greensboro Spectator*, 11 April 1985, 23.
Publisher's Weekly, 30 November 1984, 28.
Romine, Dannye. *Charlotte Observer*, 7 April 1985, 9F.
Spearman, Walter. *Danville Register*, 7 April 1985, 7E.
Vogel, Christine, *Cleveland Plain Dealer*, 17 March 1985, C–7.

Index

Willis, Newton (HBD), 17, 58, 73
Willis, Stella (HBD), 16–20, 41–42,
  63, 65, 76, 100
Winterville, North Carolina, 3, 75,
  80–81
*Women in Libraries Newsletter,
  The*, 42

"World That Winter, The," 8
Wren Jackson (NAL). *See* Jackson,
  Wren

Young adult literature, 93–96

Zindel, Paul, 14, 62, 93, 94, 95

About the Author

A former high school English and reading teacher, Ted Hipple is head of the Department of Curriculum and Instruction at the University of Tennessee, where he also teaches courses in adolescent literature. One of the founders of ALAN (the Assembly on Literature for Adolescents of the National Council of Teachers of English), he served that organization as its president in 1979 and currently is its executive secretary. He has written extensively about adolescent literature for such journals as *English Journal, College English, ALAN Review, School Counselor,* and *Techniques* and has written or edited thirteen school and college textbooks.